Cambridge Elements

Elements in Publishing and Book Culture
edited by
Samantha J. Rayner
University College London
Leah Tether
University of Bristol

ART BOOKS FOR THE PEOPLE

The Origins of The Penguin Modern Painters

David Trigg
Independent Researcher

Shaftesbury Road, Cambridge CB2 8EA, United Kingdom

One Liberty Plaza, 20th Floor, New York, NY 10006, USA

477 Williamstown Road, Port Melbourne, VIC 3207, Australia

314–321, 3rd Floor, Plot 3, Splendor Forum, Jasola District Centre,
New Delhi – 110025, India

103 Penang Road, #05–06/07, Visioncrest Commercial, Singapore 238467

Cambridge University Press is part of Cambridge University Press & Assessment,
a department of the University of Cambridge.

We share the University's mission to contribute to society through the pursuit of
education, learning and research at the highest international levels of excellence.

www.cambridge.org
Information on this title: www.cambridge.org/9781009578141

DOI: 10.1017/9781009578165

© David Trigg 2025

This publication is in copyright. Subject to statutory exception and to the provisions
of relevant collective licensing agreements, no reproduction of any part may take
place without the written permission of Cambridge University Press & Assessment.

When citing this work, please include a reference to the DOI 10.1017/9781009578165

First published 2025

A catalogue record for this publication is available from the British Library

ISBN 978-1-009-57814-1 Paperback
ISSN 2514-8524 (online)
ISSN 2514-8516 (print)

Cambridge University Press & Assessment has no responsibility for the persistence
or accuracy of URLs for external or third-party internet websites referred to in this
publication and does not guarantee that any content on such websites is, or will remain,
accurate or appropriate.

For EU product safety concerns, contact us at Calle de José Abascal, 56, 1°, 28003
Madrid, Spain, or email eugpsr@cambridge.org

Art Books for the People

The Origins of The Penguin Modern Painters

Elements in Publishing and Book Culture

DOI: 10.1017/9781009578165
First published online: July 2025

David Trigg
Independent Researcher

Author for correspondence: David Trigg, davidtrigg78@gmail.com

ABSTRACT: The Penguin Modern Painters (1944–1959) was a groundbreaking series of British art monographs designed to promote the work of contemporary artists to a general readership. In examining the factors that influenced the wartime conception and development of the series, this Element makes a contribution to the understanding of the relationship between publishing and the visual arts during the Second World War. The study argues that the emergence of The Penguin Modern Painters was inextricably linked to the aims of British wartime cultural policy and the ideology of the pre-war adult education movement. The key personalities involved are identified and their multiple and often conflicting motives analysed to provide new insights into the shifting perspectives of Britain's elites regarding the way that art was presented to the public in the 1940s. This Element provides a foundation on which further study of twentieth-century art publishing in Britain might be developed.

KEYWORDS: art books, Second World War, art publishing, Penguin Books, general reader

© David Trigg 2025

ISBNs: 9781009578141 (PB), 9781009578165 (OC)
ISSNs: 2514-8524 (online), 2514-8516 (print)

Contents

	Introduction	1
1	Propaganda and Publishing: A Pre-History of The Penguin Modern Painters	10
2	Hatching a Penguin: The Birth of The Penguin Modern Painters	21
3	Penguin and the People: Identifying an Audience for The Penguin Modern Painters	42
	Conclusion	70
	References	74

Introduction

As one of Britain's most prominent publishing houses of the twentieth century, Penguin Books is not readily associated with the production of art books. Yet, in the midst of the Second World War, it launched The Penguin Modern Painters, a groundbreaking series of nineteen short, illustrated monographs, each devoted to a single artist. As Penguin's co-founder Allen Lane (quoted in *The Bookseller*, 1944) explained, the rationale for the series was to 'make known as widely as possible, both at home and abroad, the work of our leading contemporary artists, and to show the progress which British Art had made prior to and during the war'. John Lehmann's literary miscellany *Penguin New Writing* had been promoting new literature to a general audience since November 1940, selling at its peak more than 100,000 copies an issue, and Lane was evidently hoping to achieve similar success in the field of contemporary art (Morpurgo, 1979, p. 170). His gamble paid off; the books were an immediate success and, due to their low price of just two shillings and sixpence, enjoyed sales in the tens of thousands during the latter years of the war.[1] As the British art critic Peter Fuller (1988, p. 102) commented, the series marked 'the beginning of a boom in popular art books, which has continued to this day'.

The Penguin Modern Painters initially focussed on British artists, with books on Henry Moore, Graham Sutherland, Duncan Grant, Paul Nash, Matthew Smith and John Piper appearing early on in the series. Edward Bawden, Stanley Spencer, Ben Nicholson and David Jones were added later, and then international painters, including the Swiss artist Paul Klee and the Americans Ben Shahn and Edward Hopper. An introductory text was commissioned for each book, and the list of distinguished writers included Geoffrey Grigson, Raymond Mortimer, Herbert Read, John Betjeman, Clive Bell, and Eric Newton. The sole female author was Myfanwy Evans, who was selected to introduce the work of the only woman artist in the series, Frances Hodgkins. Of the first four volumes, published in April 1944 in editions of 25,000, *Henry Moore* by Geoffrey Grigson and *Paul Nash* by Herbert Read sold out within the first month and were soon reprinted. The popularity of the

---

[1] For Penguin sales figures quoted in this Element see: Penguin Books (no date).

series led Penguin to increase the print run for subsequent titles to 40,000 copies – figures unheard of for pre-war art books.

Despite their cheap price, the books displayed no signs of compromise in terms of material quality. High-quality art paper was used throughout which, for reasons that will be explored later, was unusual for wartime publications. The popularity of the series owed much to Penguin's production values, not to mention the generous quantity of reproductions. Printed in landscape format, each book contains twelve pages of text and thirty-two plates, evenly divided between colour and black-and-white.[2] The quality of the reproductions was considered to be exceptionally good for a wartime production, and Benedict Nicolson (1946, p. 53) was not alone in judging that the series contained 'the best-coloured illustrations to be found anywhere in England at the present time'. The book reviewer of the *Manchester Guardian* (1945, p. 3) marvelled that 'such colour can be so well reproduced at so little cost', while the art critic Eric Newton (1945, p. 199) similarly noted that the reproductions were 'printed with a care that is unusual in mass-produced publication', and declared the series 'a notable landmark in the history of book production'. However, considerable momentum was lost in the late 1940s; individual titles were subject to severe delays and sales dwindled. The series struggled throughout the following decade with just three new titles published after 1950, including the final volume, *Georges Braque* by John Richardson, appearing in January 1959. Despite its drawn-out demise, the Modern Painters was an exceptional achievement for Penguin Books, being conceived and brought to market at the height of a world war, when publishers were contending with the effects of air raids, paper rationing, and fuel and staff shortages (Feather, 2006, p. 195).

Whilst the literature addressing the history and influence of Penguin Books is extensive (see, for example, Blackburn, 2020; Hare, 1995; Joicey, 1995; Kells, 2015; Morpurgo, 1979; Penguin Books, 1985; Rylance, 2005), no scholarly study of The Penguin Modern Painters has yet been

---

[2] The dimensions of the books are 22.3 x 17.8 cm. All adopt the landscape format except for *Georges Braque* by John Richardson (1959) and a revised edition of *Graham Sutherland* by Edward Sackville-West (1955), both of which retain the same dimensions but in portrait format.

published.³ A short monograph by Carol Peaker (2001) provides a general overview, but contains little critical analysis. Other discussions have tended to be fragmented and confined to individual books in the series (for instance, Button, 1993; Flynn, 2012, pp. 84–106). A couple of notable yet brief accounts by Holman (1993, 1999b) have provided useful sketches of the Modern Painters: the former in the context of wartime art publishing activities in France, Britain, and Switzerland, and the latter in relation to the wartime activities of Phaidon Press.⁴ Joicey (1995) dedicates eight pages of his PhD thesis to the topic, placing the series within a broader analysis of the cultural, political, and intellectual significance of Penguin Books between 1935 and 1956. However, the ambitious scope of his study, though making a significant contribution to Penguin studies more broadly, prevented the author from analysing the series in any significant depth.

There is, then, a lacuna in current research, but that alone does not justify this Element. The significance of the Modern Painters, both within the history of twentieth-century art publishing and the wider sociohistorical context must therefore be established. Certainly, from the vantage point of the early twenty-first century, it is difficult to fully appreciate the revolutionary nature of the series. The widespread availability of illustrated art books with informative texts and high-quality colour reproductions is today taken for granted. But in 1944, when the first four Modern Painters were published, there was simply nothing comparable. As Newton (1945) commented: 'Nothing quite like it has been done in this country before'.

That is not to say, however, that art books were unavailable before the Modern Painters. It is a common misconception that Penguin invented the mass market paperback book, but the existence of nineteenth-century sixpenny novels in Britain, dime novels in the United States and the Tauchnitz Editions in Germany gives the lie to this myth

---

³ This Element is based on material included in the author's unpublished PhD thesis, *Art Books for the People: The Penguin Modern Painters 1944–1959*, which represents the first comprehensive scholarly account of The Penguin Modern Painters. See Trigg (2017).

⁴ Holman's second article was one of the first pieces of research to make use of newly available material in the Penguin Archive at the University of Bristol.

(Schreuders, 1981). Similarly, it would be misguided to suppose that Penguin invented the contemporary art monograph. For instance, the first book devoted to the work of Henry Moore was published by the art book dealer Anton Zwemmer in 1934, a whole decade before Penguin's volume on the artist. The first book on Duncan Grant appeared even earlier, published by the Hogarth Press in 1923. Indeed, art books of one sort or another, from studies of single artists to surveys of historical periods and modern movements, were available in Britain throughout the early decades of the twentieth century.[5] However, the history of art book publishing in Britain since 1900 has still not received a scholarly overview. It is curious that art historians have been slow to embrace book history, especially considering that in the twentieth century people's knowledge of art was largely acquired through books, exhibition catalogues, and periodicals which, as Holman (1993, p. 68) notes, 'have their own distinct history'. An interest in that history underpins this Element, an aim of which is to demonstrate the value that the history of art publishing as a distinct field of study might have for historians of art.

In the absence of a definitive history of twentieth-century art book publishing in Britain, it is possible to piece together a basic overview by consulting and cross-referencing library catalogues.[6] These reveal the existence of two significant interwar series of illustrated monographs dedicated to contemporary British artists. Albert Rutherston's Contemporary British Artists was published by Ernest Benn between 1923 and 1927 and included nineteen titles on the work of artists such as Augustus John, Stanley Spencer, Jacob Epstein, and Eric Gill. This was followed by The Fleuron's British Artists of To-Day (1925–29), of which seven volumes were published, featuring Mark Gertler, John Nash, Gilbert Spencer, Frank

---

[5] 'Art books' broadly defined existed well before 1800, though the history of such publications remains scant. On the beginnings of art publishing see Haskell (1987).

[6] See, for instance, https://discover.libraryhub.jisc.ac.uk which brings together the catalogues of nearly one hundred major UK and Irish libraries. On the history of art book publishing in the twentieth century see Holman (2024); Nyburg (2014); Halliday (1991); Craker (1985).

Dobson, Paul Nash, Duncan Grant, and H. H. Newton.[7] These two series, which have yet to be studied and whose history is beyond the scope of this study, stand as important precursors to The Penguin Modern Painters. The 1930s saw far less activity. As Holman (1999a, p. 311) writes, 'the majority of books then published in England were introductions to art appreciation, attempts to spread an understanding of Modernism, or overviews of a national school of painting, and the number of books devoted each year to an individual artist or movement could be counted on the fingers of one hand'.[8] More work needs to be done in this area, though it is known that Zwemmer's Henry Moore monograph, printed in an edition of just fifteen hundred, sold dismally with just a little over twenty copies being bought in the first few years following publication (Halliday, 1991, p. 212; Berthoud, 2003, pp. 135–37).[9] This lack of success was largely due to the fact that Zwemmer had no machinery for distribution, taking it upon himself to personally visit London's bookshops to promote the six-shilling book.[10] He soon discovered, as did the publisher Stanley Unwin in 1937, that 'booksellers seem to be obsessed with the idea that there is no market in England for art books' (Stanley Unwin to Béla Horovitz, 10 March 1937, quoted in Holman, 1999a, p. 313).

What makes The Penguin Modern Painters so distinctive and worthy of study is the innovative nature of the series, which differed considerably from the many publications preceding it. Firstly, the books were paperback,

---

[7] In addition to these was The Bodley Head's Masters of Modern Art series (1925–28), though its seventeen volumes featured mainly Impressionists and Post-Impressionists from outside of Britain.

[8] Phaidon books were produced in England from 1938, though it was not until 1943 that the firm's first monograph dedicated to a living British artist appeared: *Augustus John* by John Rothenstein.

[9] The book was only saved from complete disaster by a number of orders from Japan where proponents of the country's Surrealist movement were beginning to take an interest in Moore's work.

[10] At one point Zwemmer even approached Allen Lane, who at the time was working as a travelling salesman for the Bodley Head, and he persuaded him to include the book among his samples.

a format unheard of for contemporary art monographs.[11] Secondly, at two shillings and sixpence, they were remarkably cheap when compared, for example, with Phaidon's hardback monographs, which in 1944 sold for twenty shillings each.[12] Indeed, Lund Humphries's revised edition of Zwemmer's Henry Moore monograph, published a month after the first Modern Painters, was priced at an exorbitant three pounds and three shillings. Thirdly, these books were printed in extremely large editions. Intended for the mass market, they were accordingly available for purchase in unconventional outlets; one did not have to enter a foreboding bookshop but could easily pick up a copy from the local Woolworth's, railway bookstall or W. H. Smith newsagents (Mandler, 2019). Lastly, the series was innovative in its choice of artists and was responsible for publishing the first ever monographs on the work of Graham Sutherland, Ben Nicholson, Matthew Smith, John Piper, Edward Burra, Victor Pasmore, Edward Bawden, Ben Shahn, Frances Hodgkins, David Jones, and Ivon Hitchens. The Modern Painters stands as a remarkable development in art book publishing, but perhaps the most intriguing aspect of the project is that it emerged during wartime.

When Allen Lane and his brothers began Penguin in 1935 they could not have imagined that nearly a decade later their firm would be publishing contemporary art books. Driven by a desire to make book ownership accessible to all, their priority at the outset had been the introduction of inexpensive paperback editions of quality modern literature. As Lane (1938, p. 969) stated, the initial aim was to provide 'good books cheap' and to that end he 'staked everything upon it'. In his history of Penguin Books, Stuart Kells (2015, p. 184) has suggested that the Modern Painters, being conceived and brought to market during the Second World War, was an 'oddly timed series'. On the face of it, Lane's decision to pursue an ambitious series of art books in wartime certainly seems extraordinary. Whilst the appetite for reading was soaring (Rylance, 2005, p. 49), many in the publishing

---

[11] Exhibition catalogues were commonly printed with paper covers but The Penguin Modern Painters was the first series of contemporary art monographs to be published in the paperback format.

[12] As advertised in *The Bookseller*, 24 February 1944.

industry found themselves fighting for survival, and though Penguin was in an advantageous position regarding paper quotas (as we shall see), the publisher had no prior experience in the field of art book publishing.[13]

How, then, do we account for the appearance of The Penguin Modern Painters during the Second World War? This Element seeks to understand the multiple factors that led Lane to bring the series to market. It considers the social, political, and cultural context in which the series was conceived, the forces that shaped its development and its place within the trajectory of Penguin Books during this period. From this, further questions arise: to what extent did the wartime context influence the conception of the series? What convinced Lane of its marketability? What were the preconditions for determining its success? What challenges did Penguin face in preparing the books for market? Who was its target audience and how successful was Penguin in reaching this market? In pursuing these questions, this Element provides an important prehistory of The Penguin Modern Painters, arguing that the series owes its existence as much to the climate in which it emerged as it does to the tenacity and personal ambition of Allen Lane. Its case study-based approach demonstrates the significance of the books to discussions surrounding the visual arts, publishing, and art education during the 1930s and 1940s while making a contribution to Penguin studies more broadly and the nascent field of scholarship addressing the intersection of book history and art history.

The Penguin Modern Painters was one of many new series launched by Lane's firm during the war. By the time the first volumes went on sale, Penguin was well on the way to establishing itself as the nation's popular educator, providing high-quality, inexpensive books to a huge readership. The series emerged alongside several other wartime initiatives that sought to promote the work of Britain's artists to a broad public. The majority of these were Government supported and specifically designed to boost public morale and nurture popular taste. As Weight (1995, p. 42) has observed, a consensus emerged among the nation's cultural and political elites that 'the arts, if properly planned, had a vital role to play in postwar Britain'. This was a driving factor in the creation of the state-sponsored War Artists'

---

[13] On wartime publishing in England see Holman (2008).

Advisory Committee (WAAC), the chair of which was Sir Kenneth Clark, one of the most powerful figures in the British art world who was director of the National Gallery and chosen as general editor of The Penguin Modern Painters.

The WAAC was established by Clark in 1939 and operated under the auspices of the Ministry of Information (MoI). Its stated aim was to compile a comprehensive visual record of the war and as such represented an important source of support for artists. Clark, who had become an influential patron in the 1930s, saw the WAAC as a way of continuing his patronage in wartime with the support of the state. As he claimed in later life, his intention 'was simply to keep artists at work on any pretext, and, as far as possible, to prevent them from being killed' (Clark, 1977, p. 22). However, his personal preference for figurative modes of representation led him to privilege artists working in styles that were visually conservative and resistant to the supposed extremes of international modernism.[14] Seven of the WAAC's artists were included in The Penguin Modern Painters, and, as Section 1 will show, the links between the WAAC, the British state and Penguin are significant.[15] Drawing on unpublished material in the Penguin Archive, War Artists Archive, Kenneth Clark papers and the Ministry of Information papers, this section examines the role that Clark and his committee played in the conception of the series.

As will be shown, the extraordinary success that Penguin enjoyed during the war, coupled with the remarkable surge of public interest in the visual arts, provided a firm basis for a new series of art books. Section 2 examines three key areas that were fundamental to the success of the project: the immediate social and cultural context, in particular the wartime demand for books and increasingly books about art; the advantageous position that Penguin found itself in and the reasons why the firm was so well placed to produce such an ambitious series, and, lastly, the role of Lane's personal ambitions in the area of illustrated books. The section also considers the progenitorial role of

---

[14] On the extent to which the Modern Painters embodied Clark's aesthetic values, see Trigg (2017, chapters 3 and 4).

[15] The artists were: Edward Bawden, Paul Nash, Graham Sutherland, John Piper, Duncan Grant, Henry Moore, and Stanley Spencer.

Art Books for the People

Penguin's Editor-in-Chief, W. E. Williams, the significance of Lane's appointment of Kenneth Clark as general editor, and the multiple production challenges faced by Penguin's staff.

Williams viewed his position at Penguin as an extension of his activities in the adult education movement. His great enthusiasm for the Modern Painters lay in his desire to foster aesthetic appreciation and develop new audiences for art – objectives he had been pursuing since the mid-1930s. Recognising the potential of the Modern Painters to expand this work, he championed the enterprise and was instrumental in defining its target audience. Section 3 seeks to understand the identity of that intended readership. It assesses how successful Penguin was in reaching it while giving consideration to the way that the books addressed those readers. By examining the relationship between Williams's involvement in Penguin and his various activities in the field of adult education, the section questions the extent to which The Penguin Modern Painters should be seen as part of a larger project to establish a post-war common culture.

1 Propaganda and Publishing: A Pre-History of The Penguin Modern Painters

1.1 The War Artists' Advisory Committee

In November 1940, two years before work began on The Penguin Modern Painters, Allen Lane met with Kenneth Clark to discuss a proposed series of books that the WAAC was hoping to publish with Penguin to achieve wider appreciation for the artworks commissioned by the committee. Although exhibitions became the principal vehicle by which the WAAC promoted its collection during the war, plans for some form of official publication had been mooted as early as November 1939. It was Noel Carrington, the book designer and commissioning editor at Country Life, who first suggested to Clark that his committee should publish a monthly periodical devoted to war artists (WAAC, 1939a). During the First World War, a ten-part government-sanctioned series titled *The Western Front* featuring war drawings by Muirhead Bone had been published between December 1916 and October 1917. A further four books promoting the work of C. R. W. Nevinson, Paul Nash, Eric Kennington and John Lavery appeared towards the end of the War titled *British Artists at the Front*. These were published 'from the offices of Country Life' at the behest of the Propaganda Bureau at Wellington House.[16] Priced at five shillings, they were printed in large editions and aimed at an urban middle class.

With this precedent there was an expectation within the MoI that the work of the WAAC's artists would be reproduced in popular newspapers and magazines, as well as in the form of postcards (WAAC, 1939b). Clark, however, envisaged a far more deluxe proposal. His vision was for a 'fine periodical' that would be 'so attractively produced that it should readily be bought for its own sake' (Clark quoted in WAAC, 1939a). Clark surmised that since the circulation of art magazines was likely to be limited during the war, a natural market for a 'first-rate publication' would be found among the intelligentsia. This speaks to Clark's conception of his committee's core audience during the early months of the war: a small and cultured elite

---

[16] The Propaganda Bureau oversaw the official War Artists programme during the First World War. On this topic, see Malvern (2004, pp. 17–35).

upon whom war art would likely have its greatest impact as propaganda. A wider public, he surmised, could be reached via cheap, illustrated papers such as *Picture Post* but, for the select audience that he wished to target, a luxury publication 'would be useful propaganda, especially since some of those who would buy it might be the very people who needed a stimulus'. Clark was concerned that this group was perhaps more predisposed to apathy or even defeatism than other sections of the population and reasoned that a sumptuous publication of war art could boost morale.

As Foss (1991, pp. 61–62) has shown, the perceived propaganda value of war art was essential to the survival of the WAAC, which justified its existence and funding from the MoI on this basis. Publicly, Clark was careful to distance his committee from such activities. In Britain, propaganda was perceived to be profoundly undemocratic and associated with Germany's Ministry of Popular Enlightenment and Propaganda, which had been established soon after the Nazi Party took power in 1933. As one correspondent to *New Statesman and Nation* put it: 'the Government should recognise that in this country propaganda "won't wash." Goebbels has stolen all the thunder' (Checksfield, 1940). Writing in *The Listener* during the second month of the war, Clark (1939b) warned that an artist engaged in the production of propaganda would likely 'coarsen his style and degrade his vision'. But the WAAC was placed within the MoI, the government department responsible for sustaining civilian morale, and therefore necessarily implicated in the production of propaganda. Indeed, the MoI's Director of General Production, Robert Alexander Bevan (1940), informed Clark that the WAAC's publication proposals 'were not designed to emphasise the art side of the venture but to bring the art definitely into the service of propaganda'.

Unlike *The Western Front*, which had been published in editions of 30,000, Clark intended his publication to number just 5,000 copies (WAAC, 1940a). In targeting a narrow demographic he was echoing a policy developed during the First World War, that cultural propaganda aimed at educated, opinion-forming intellectuals could be effective in shaping public attitudes. In the words of one government official (Ministry of National Service, 1918): 'It is better to influence those who can influence others than attempt a direct appeal to the mass of the population.' In November 1939, it was the belief in a trickle-down approach to propaganda that drove Clark's ambition for his 'first-rate publication' which, he hoped, would not only be sponsored but actually produced by the Government (WAAC, 1939a). However, when Clark met with Lane a year later, the proposal under discussion was for a very different kind of publication, one aimed not at a small elite but a general audience. The involvement of Penguin, which had made its name by introducing high-quality paperback fiction and non-fiction to the mass market, indicates that Clark's views regarding government-produced publications had shifted considerably. His change in thinking was a result of the MoI's rejection of his plans for an influential periodical. As Head of Publications, William Surrey Dane (1939), had written: 'I do not think a publication of this nature would have a very big sale and surely there would hardly be sufficient paintings and posters to justify a separate publication'.[17] Others concurred, and at a meeting about copyright and reproduction arrangements there was general agreement that it would be difficult to justify to the Treasury either the expense or the allocation of paper to such a proposal (WAAC, 1939b). Clark, however, did not completely give up on his deluxe publication and continued to advocate for it despite a lack of support from colleagues.

The MoI was now hoping to pursue a popular publication that would target a wide public. It was suggested that a series of illustrated shilling books should be published: thematic collections of war art dealing with specific topics (WAAC, 1939b). Reminiscent of *British Artists at the Front*, they were to be cheap, mass-produced publications aimed at a popular audience rather than a small, select group. This attitude reflected a fundamental shift in the MoI's position. The notion that a publication of war art would have its greatest impact if aimed at influential individuals had given way to a belief in addressing a mass readership directly. As the war progressed, the MoI became increasingly favourable towards supporting illustrated books aimed at a popular readership and began working directly with commercial publishers, clandestinely sponsoring books that it did not want the public to perceive as propaganda. A notable example of the Ministry working in this way was the illustrated series Britain in Pictures, which originated from within the MoI but was published by William Collins. Instigated in 1940 by former BBC

[17] Dane was Managing Director of Odhams Press before being seconded to the MoI, first as Head of Publications and then Controller of the General Production Division.

producer Hilda Matheson, the series was conceived as a propaganda scheme to promote 'the British way of life in all its varied colour' (Keir, 1952, p. 267) and its eighty-plus titles included *Life Among the English* by Rose Macaulay (1942), *British Romantic Artists* by John Piper (1942) and *English Cities and Small Towns* by John Betjeman (1943). Macaulay's book, which featured war art by Henry Moore and Anthony Gross, was described by *The Bookseller* (Squire, 1942) as 'a highly important contribution to the national war effort'.[18]

1.2 The Books and Pamphlets Programme of the Ministry of Information

The shilling books on war art that Clark discussed with Lane were, like Britain in Pictures, to be supported by the MoI as part of its Books and Pamphlets Programme, which encouraged and sometimes instigated books highlighting positive episodes from British history, British cultural heritage, or anything with an underlying message to which the Ministry was sympathetic. As Holman (2008, p. 102) observes, such propaganda 'was most effective when least visible, that is, when it appeared to be produced and distributed by a trade publisher with no connection to the Government'. The Ministry supported publishers in one of three ways: 'joining subject to author and author to suitable publisher; supporting the book with publicity; supplying paper from the Ministry's ration' (Ministry of Information, 1940). The latter was especially enticing for publishers who were struggling with the impact of paper rationing that had come into force in February 1940 with the Government's Control of Paper Order. As one government official (Parrish, 1940) put it:

> if the Ministry can be relied upon to obtain paper for publications it is prepared to sponsor, then the whole book and periodical trade will be eager under present conditions

---

[18] Priced at four shillings and sixpence, the Britain in Pictures books were nearly twice the price of The Penguin Modern Painters, but this did not dampen sales; in a 1944 advertisement for the series, Collins reported that there was an 'overwhelming demand' for the books, which had forced the publisher to sell the series on a strict quota basis; see *The Bookseller*, 16 November 1944, p. 483.

to work in line with the Ministry and to take the maximum commercial risk in order to obtain the business.

The Britain in Pictures project set an important precedent for the MoI. Not only did it demonstrate the kind of effective partnership that could be forged between state and publisher but also the great potential of illustrated books. In fact, illustrated books were perceived to be so important for the Ministry that its head of publications, Robert Fraser (1941), urged they become a central concern of the Books and Pamphlets Programme:

> The book is not an easy medium of propaganda to handle. In wartime, propagandists must aim at securing broad mass effects relatively quickly. [...] From that certain other decisions take themselves. The book must be cheap. Its treatment must be dramatic, human, lively. It must, above all, use pictures. Indeed, it must so use pictures as to become two books in one – a picture book and a text book – and it must carry the full propaganda message once in the text and for a second time in the pictures and captions which together must tell the continuous story to those who will not read continuous text. It seems that when these qualities are added to a good manuscript which has the status of being *official*, propaganda best sellers can be created.

Fraser's vivid description of propaganda books that carefully balanced word and image must surely have resonated with Clark and his committee, encouraging them to push forward with their publishing plans.

A table produced by the MoI's Publications Division (Ministry of Information, 1941) shows that it was sponsoring forthcoming books and pamphlets for, among others, Hodder and Stoughton, Faber and Faber, OUP and Methuen. Although Penguin was not on this list, the firm had previously received six tons of paper for the Puffin Picture Books, a new educational series designed to inform children about everyday topics such as natural history, technology, agriculture and the built environment. The first four titles, which were all war-themed, were printed in runs of 10,000 and promptly sold out.[19] The Ministry clearly recognised the role that Penguin could play in influencing public opinion, and, just a few days after the outbreak of war, it made a secret agreement with Lane to produce a series of threepenny propaganda pamphlets that would include titles such as *The Science of War* and *War Aims* (Ministry of Information, 1939). However, this provisional arrangement inexplicably came to nothing and the titles were instead given to other publishers.[20] For example, a book on naval power by Sir Herbert Richmond that Penguin had been asked to produce in October 1939 appeared the following year as *The Naval Role in Modern Warfare* published as part of the Oxford Pamphlets of World Affairs series. This did not discourage Lane, however, who continued to pursue his own war-themed books, with titles including *The Real Cost of the War* and *Science in War* (both published in 1940 as Penguin Specials).[21] Lane's propensity to forge ahead with an idea, whether or not he found wider support for it, was characteristic of the way in which he ran Penguin during this period and would soon prove instrumental for the early development of The Penguin Modern Painters.

1.3 The Road to Penguin

Despite the Ministry's early interest in Penguin and its support for the illustrated Puffin Picture Books, Lane's firm was not its first choice to publish the WAAC's shilling books. The MoI initially approached His Majesty's Stationery Office (HMSO), which acted as official publishers to the Ministry. Its Director of Publications, C. F. S. Plumbley, was keen to secure the contract but Clark was indignant at the suggestion, declaring that he 'could not submit modern artists to the indignity of seeing their work badly reproduced' (Clark, 1941a). He mistrusted the Stationery Office, doubting the quality of its work, and made it known to the MoI that he believed it was 'for his committee to take

---

[19] They included *War on Land*, *War at Sea*, *War in the Air* and *On the Farm* (originally proposed as *War on the Farm*).

[20] No explanation for this could be found within extant MoI files.

[21] One of Penguin's most visible contributions to the war effort was The Forces Book Club, which provided cheap literature to the troops. However, despite being officially sanctioned, the scheme failed to attract the ongoing support of the War Office and it folded after just eleven months; see Pearson (1996).

the initiative in making recommendations as to how reproductions should be issued' (Dickey, 1939).[22] The WAAC (1940b) decided instead to approach OUP, a trusted publisher to whom they had previously proposed a book on the subject of Bomber Command with reproductions of paintings by Paul Nash, Eric Kennington, and William Rothenstein.

For Clark, a key reason for working with OUP was the hope that, in addition to producing the shilling books, the publisher might also produce his longed-for deluxe periodical of war art, which, he likely hoped, would help foster patronage and support for the nation's artists. His enthusiasm for this project led him to prepare an ambitious forty-eight-page dummy, showing that the proposed publication was to be richly illustrated in both colour and black-and-white, and would employ a range of printing processes (WAAC, 1940a). The prestigious OUP name would no doubt have appealed to his intended readership: an elite group of art collectors, connoisseurs, and educated laymen who, like Clark himself, took art seriously and were interested in supporting artists, especially during wartime. However, OUP communicated that it was 'lukewarm' to the suggestion and expressed ambivalence about taking on either project (Dickey, 1940a). Undeterred, the WAAC continued its search for a suitable publisher.

Another firm that the WAAC (1940c) had hoped to work with was the Curwen Press, a respected publisher renowned for its high-quality books and art prints.[23] In the summer of 1940, plans were afoot to produce with Curwen a portfolio of lithographs by Eric Ravilious, but, in the face of paper shortages, the Treasury's subsequent ban on 'luxury' printing had halted the project (WAAC, 1940d). In a bid to secure a cheaper form of reproduction, the committee sought the advice of Robert Wellington, an expert in the art of lithography who in 1937 had collaborated with John Piper to launch a series of large, affordable, poster-like prints under the

---

[22] Unlike in the First World War, HMSO could now act as an independent publishing firm and was recognised as such by the Publishers Association and the Booksellers Association; much of its work came from Government departments.

[23] Many well-known graphic artists worked with Curwen during the 1930s, and the firm had been responsible for printing the Fleuron's British Artists of To-Day series in the 1920s. See Powers (2008).

name Contemporary Lithographs.[24] It transpired that Wellington was collaborating with Penguin Books to produce two volumes in its new King Penguin series: one on English churches by John Piper and the other on zoo animals by the sculptor and equine painter John Skeaping.[25] The King Penguins were small, illustrated reference books featuring sixteen full-colour reproductions with thirty pages of text that sold for just one shilling, which although twice as expensive as regular Penguins, still represented extraordinary value for money.[26] Sensing an opportunity for the WAAC, the committee's secretary, Edward Montgomery O'Rorke Dickey (1940b), suggested to Clark that the King Penguin format 'might be the very thing for some of our war artists work'. The committee agreed and Lane was soon invited to put together a proposition.

Lane promptly sent the best examples of colour printing he had: The King Penguins and Puffin Picture Books. The quality of reproduction in these publications greatly impressed Clark, but others in the WAAC worried that colour printing would prove prohibitively expensive and so it was suggested that monochrome booklets be produced instead. Lane assured Clark that, for an editorial cost of £100 per volume, Penguin could produce a book along the lines of The King Penguins with up to thirty-two pages of black-and-white photogravures to be sold at sixpence, or slightly more than double that size if they were priced at one shilling. Alternatively, a shilling book modelled after the Puffins could be produced, which would include both colour and black-and-white plates. He also suggested that this proposal would look better if the books were oriented in landscape rather than portrait (a format that would eventually be adopted for the Modern Painters). Clark informed Lane in December 1940 that the King Penguin format was just what the WAAC wanted. The two men met a few days later and it was decided that each book should be devoted to a single subject, contain forty-eight black-and-white plates with sixteen pages of text, and be

---

[24] On Contemporary Lithographs, see Artmonsky (2007).

[25] These books were never published.

[26] The King Penguins were modelled after Insel Verlag's *Insel-Bücherei* (Island Library), an affordable and beautifully designed series of illustrated books published in Leipzig from 1912. See Lake (2014).

published as part of the King Penguin series (WAAC, 1940e). Lane was to pay the MoI £50 per volume for the right to reproduce works from the WAAC's collection and Clark insisted that no expenses of any sort should fall on the Ministry, nor would there be any obligations for them to purchase or publicise the books.

Towards the end of 1940, Lane sent the WAAC a tentative and rather fanciful list of proposed authors for the series that had been devised during a Penguin editorial meeting. H.M. The Queen, or perhaps Lord Reith, it was suggested, could pen texts on the Blitz, while Lloyd George might write on the topic of wartime supply. War heroes such as Sir Wyndham Deedes and Sir Roger Keyes might be approached to write about civil defence and the war at sea, while the Home Secretary, Herbert Morrison, could tackle the subject of air-raid shelters.[27] Such suggestions may reveal more about Lane's perception of Clark than anything else; the majority of proposed authors on the curious list – notably devoid of art historians, critics, and artists – were, like Clark himself, elite, establishment figures. Nevertheless, it seemed that at last, with the help of Penguin Books, the WAAC would have its official publication. The committee's objective now was 'to aim at the widest possible circulation for really satisfactory books of reproductions at popular prices' (WAAC, 1940f). But Clark, who was still harbouring a desire to pursue a luxury publication, decided that OUP should be given another opportunity to compete for the contract, reasoning to his committee that 'each firm should have an equal chance to show what they can do' (Dickey, 1940c).

When OUP learned of Penguin's involvement, the firm experienced a sudden change of heart and promptly informed the WAAC that it was now 'most anxious' to undertake the work 'on the most advantageous terms possible' (Clark, 1941b). Additionally, OUP made it known that, alongside the shilling books, it was willing also to produce a larger, deluxe publication with two hundred reproductions to be sold for seven shillings and sixpence. With two publishers now vying for the shilling books, Clark was, he claimed, compelled to put the two offers to the WAAC who, after 'careful

---

[27] Herbert Morrison had lent his name to the eponymous indoor air-raid shelter that had been designed to protect people from falling bricks and masonry.

consideration', chose OUP for the sole reason that the publisher had agreed to the more comprehensive deluxe volume. 'I know that this decision will be a disappointment to you,' Clark wrote to Lane (Clark, 1941b), emphasising his gratefulness for the enthusiasm he had shown. Perhaps wishing to distance himself from the decision, he added that it was not for him to question his committee. This episode illustrates well Clark's mercurial personality; though he had clearly warmed to Lane's proposal and had much sympathy with Penguin's broader democratising mission, the stature, reputation, and history of OUP were ostensibly far more alluring to this establishment figure and his WAAC colleagues.

1.4 War Pictures by British Artists

The WAAC's shilling books were published by OUP in May 1942 under the title War Pictures by British Artists, but when compared with Penguin's illustrated publications, the slim pocket books appear markedly inferior: the black-and-white images are small, have a limited tonal range and many are printed on their sides in order to fit the books' narrow portrait orientation (19 × 12 cm). Priced at one shilling and threepence, the four titles – *War at Sea*, *Blitz*, *R.A.F.*, and *Army* – were issued in editions of 25,000 and sold out in less than a year.[28] Each slim, sixty-four-page paperback contains a concise introductory essay followed by around fifty black-and-white reproductions with summary annotations. Their success led to a second four-volume series – *Women*, *Production*, *Soldiers*, and *Air Raid* – which was published in November 1943 in editions of 20,000 and priced one shilling and sixpence. Yet while their success was welcomed by the WAAC, their mode of presentation must surely have disappointed Clark. The standard of the books could not have escaped the attention of Lane either, for it was just a few weeks after the first four volumes were published that he wrote to Clark introducing his concept for a new series of art books that would become The Penguin Modern Painters. Lane knew, and had proved to Clark, that Penguin was capable of producing a far superior

---

[28] On the War Pictures by British Artists series see Llewellyn and Liss (2016). Sales figures are recorded in ledgers held by the Oxford University Press Archive: LO/CA/003676(CA53); LO/CA/003697–99(CA54); LO/CA/003700–4 (CA54).

product than the WAAC had achieved with OUP, though it was not until he actually set eyes on the War Pictures by British Artists books that he felt compelled to begin planning his own series, one that would not be propagandistic but focussed on individual artists.

Before his contact with the WAAC, Lane had shown no interest in pursuing art monographs, and the extent of his engagement with contemporary art lay primarily in commissioning artists to provide illustrations for his King Penguin and Puffin Picture Books. But, as an astute businessman, he clearly sensed an opportunity in 1942 and perhaps even wanted to corner the market before OUP could publish the larger, luxury volume of war artists' work. However, producing a series of art monographs under wartime conditions and without government support still presented a challenge, especially considering that Penguin had no experience in art book publishing and Lane himself had little knowledge of the field. What, then, were the factors that convinced him of the marketability of The Penguin Modern Painters and what were the preconditions for determining its success? To answer these questions, the next section will examine three key areas: the immediate social and cultural context, the performance of Penguin Books during the war and the role of Lane's personal ambition.

2 Hatching a Penguin: The Birth of The Penguin Modern Painters

Kenneth Clark was delighted to learn of Lane's proposal for a new art book series. 'To judge from the amount of interest of which I have evidence during the last year,' he remarked, 'I think they would go well' (Clark, 1942a). There was indeed a remarkable and unprecedented amount of public interest in the arts during the Second World War. As one journalist (*North Devon Journal-Herald*, 1942) observed, 'when the war came there was a consistent and increasing demand by the people in all parts of England for the entail and spiritual enjoyment to be found in music, art, and drama'. Galleries were bustling, concert halls and theatres were full to overflowing, and there was a significant demand for books. As John Lehmann (1960, p. 161) later remarked: 'It seemed to me – as it seemed to many others – that under the most unlikely conditions, in the middle of a total war, something of a renaissance of the arts was taking place.' Nowhere was this more acute than in the realm of the visual arts.

2.1 The Popularity of Wartime Exhibitions

At the beginning of the war, Clark had sent the priceless treasures of the National Gallery to Manod Quarry, near Blaenau Ffestiniog in Wales, to protect them from aerial attacks. The Gallery's empty walls provided the perfect venue to showcase the WAAC's growing collection of war art, and a continually evolving exhibition was displayed there from July 1940 to May 1945. It proved so successful with the public that in 1941 a decision was made to open the galleries on Sunday afternoons to accommodate the crowds. As *The Scotsman* reported in 1943: 'no matter what the hour, the galleries containing the pictures by war artists are always full of animated little groups of people, who do not hesitate to express their pleasure frankly' (L.M.W., 1943). This was in marked contrast to the pre-war years when attendance was so low that one's 'footsteps would echo through the quiet rooms'. The popularity of the exhibition was captured in Jill Craigie's documentary film about Britain's war artists, *Out of Chaos* (1944), the opening scenes of which show crowds of people streaming into the gallery on a Saturday afternoon.

The popularity of the war artists' exhibition can, of course, be largely attributed to the topicality of the work on display. But the new public interest in art was certainly not limited to pictures dealing with war themes. According to the *Daily Mail*'s George Edinger (1943, p. 2), the National Gallery exhibition '19th Century French Paintings' (11 December 1942–17 January 1943) attracted 40,000 visitors during its five-week run, and on at least two occasions the gallery doors 'had to be shut in the face of a long and disappointed queue'. The new surge of interest in the visual arts was not limited to London. At the National Gallery of Scotland and the National Museum of Wales, temporary wartime exhibitions attracted three or four times the number of visitors than the pre-war average (Richardson, 1995, p. 93). Nine touring exhibitions of paintings from the WAAC's collection were exhibited in more than one hundred British villages, towns, and cities, generating a remarkable amount of interest and, as Foss (2007, pp. 183–84) notes, setting visitor attendance records at many venues.

Four of the WAAC's touring exhibitions were organised by the British Institute of Adult Education (BIAE) as part of its Art for the People scheme, which had been established by W. E. Williams in 1935 to provide free exhibitions for people living in towns and cities without access to art galleries. During the war, the scheme was run in association with the Council for the Encouragement of Music and the Arts (CEMA), the State-funded forerunner of the Arts Council of Great Britain. In 1940, exhibitions were successfully toured by CEMA and the BIAE to eighty venues, attracting over 300,000 visitors (Williams, 1941, p. 4). In 1941, ninety-three venues hosted popular touring exhibitions including several large thematic shows that included 'British Landscape Tradition, 1740–1940', 'Contemporary British Painting', and 'British Watercolours and Drawings, 1900–1940'.[29] There was much excitement surrounding these exhibitions. The *Somerset County Herald* (1941) described the exhibition 'British Landscape Tradition' as 'the finest and most comprehensive exhibition of pictures ever seen in this part of the country [. . .] it is doubtful whether even in London a better collection could be found at this time'. Such enthusiastic responses were repeated across the country, and

---

[29] One of the largest exhibitions, 'The Artist at Work', was subsequently adapted into a popular Penguin paperback of the same name by Helmut Ruhemann in 1951.

the number of recorded attendances at these exhibitions that year totalled 367,000 (Williams, 1971, p. 21). In light of this, the prospect of publishing art monographs must have seemed to Lane like a fortuitous business opportunity. But it was not just the consistently large attendances at free art exhibitions that convinced him of the marketability of The Penguin Modern Painters (for that alone was no guarantee of sales); rather, it was another aspect of the cultural renaissance: the unexpected demand for books about art.

2.2 The Wartime Demand for Art Books

Despite paper shortages and diminishing stock, overall book sales in Britain actually rose between 1939 and 1945. As Stanley Unwin (1944, pp. 17–18) commented, 'the curious thing is that though they are advertised less, the demand for books is greater than it has ever been before. The war has turned publishing completely topsy-turvy'. As Joseph McAleer (1992, pp. 62–63) records, in 1941 eighty-six new bookshops opened their doors and borrowing from libraries increased by 15 per cent. The Central Statistical Office recorded that expenditure on books, newspapers and magazines increased from £64 million in 1938 to £67 million in 1943, and £77 million in 1945. This trend, which was no doubt an encouragement to Lane, reflected the fact that unemployment became virtually non-existent during this period and, consequently, personal income rose by almost 100 per cent between 1938 and 1945, creating a climate in which cultural products could thrive.[30] A further boost to Lane came when booksellers began noting a marked increase in demand for books on art. As Anton Zwemmer reported to his son in August 1943:

> [I]n spite of the scarcity, we sell more than ever and the 10 months' trading ending end July showed that we have surpassed last year's figures and incidentally we will this year pass any prewar figure [...] No catalogues, no advertising, people just come along and mill around and spend. (quoted in Halliday, 1991, p. 192)

---

[30] See Hancock (1951, p. 200, table 181).

Before the war, general booksellers had shown little interest in stocking art books, believing there to be no market for them. Phaidon's British distributor had experienced great difficulty in convincing bookshops to stock the publisher's art monographs in the late 1930s. During the war, however, market conditions changed to such an extent that, as early as 1941, Unwin could tell Phaidon's co-founder Béla Horovitz that the book trade was realising that 'Phaidons are safe stock' (Unwin to Horovitz, 3 March 1941, quoted in Holman, 1999a, p. 325). The public's hunger for publications about art was also seen at the National Gallery where sales of the cheap, illustrated guide booklets accompanying the 'British War Artists' exhibition exceeded all expectations. In July 1940, 400 copies were sold on a single day (Dickey, 1940d). The interest in art books was, as with exhibitions, not limited to war-themed titles. Christina Foyle, director of Foyle's bookshop in London, responded to the demand for art books by starting the Foyle's Art Book Club.[31] When she contacted OUP in 1943 requesting recommendations for her new club, Humphrey Milford dutifully offered her two war-themed titles that had been published the previous year: *Men of the R.A.F.* by William Rothenstein and *Drawing the R.A.F.* by Eric Kennington (Milford, 1943). However, Foyle considered these to be too specialised for her readers. Whilst the members of her club desired art books, there was evidently little hunger for topical, war-related publications, especially not ones filled with portraits of R.A.F. servicemen.

The wartime enthusiasm for the visual arts, the demand for art books, and the success of the War Pictures by British Artists series must have convinced Lane of a healthy market for art monographs. The scheme he had in mind, however, was far more ambitious than the morale-boosting, war-themed booklets published by OUP. The scope of the Modern Painters was to be much broader; each book was to be dedicated to an individual artist and would contain pre-war work as well as wartime commissions. Furthermore, unlike OUP's low-quality monochrome reproductions, these were to include

---

[31] Book clubs were subscription services through which members could obtain books at cheaper prices. One of the most famous examples is Victor Gollancz's Left Book Club. Foyles ran several genre-specific book clubs, including the Travel Book Club and Scientific Book Club.

copies each (Kitchin, 1938, p. 972). The firm's success, which would significantly impact the future availability of books in Britain, came too late to save The Bodley Head from liquidation, but proved to the trade the benefits of engaging with the 'new reading public'.

The decision to proceed with the Penguin concept in the face of opposition and uncertainty demonstrates the tenacity with which Lane, eminently confident in his own abilities, ran his firm during its early years. The Penguin Modern Painters was, of course, a radically different proposal to the cheap paperback reprints that had launched Penguin in 1935, but the series was not entirely without precedent. As Lane's former employee and biographer J. E. Morpurgo (1979, pp. 128, 143) noted, the publisher was 'always most contented when pioneering', and it was not long before he began to pursue other modes of publishing, remaining 'devoted to the idea that somehow he must enlarge the Penguin range to include illustrated books'. It was an ambition that he had inherited from his uncle John at The Bodley Head, whose conviction was that books must not only satisfy the mind, but also the eye.

The first of Lane's publications to include illustrations were the Pelican Books, a parallel non-fiction imprint launched in 1937 that was designed as an avowedly educational series. Pelicans were marketed to students, teachers, and readers enrolled in adult education classes such as those organised by the Workers' Educational Association (WEA). The list was representative of the best in adult education, offering books on a range of subjects including history, science, politics, economics and the arts. The books, which were produced in the same format as Penguins, sold in significantly lower quantities, but individual titles could still sell in the tens of thousands. It was deemed essential that Pelicans dealing with the visual arts should include illustrations. Two notable examples appeared in 1938: *Art in England*, a selection of essays compiled by R. S. Lambert on the centenary of John Constable's death, and *Modern German Art* by Peter Thoene, a Pelican Special responding to the Nazis' 'Degenerate Art Exhibition' and scheduled to coincide with the 'Twentieth Century German Art' exhibition at the New Burlington Galleries that year.[37] These publications, with their low-quality,

[37] Peter Thoene was a pseudonym of the Yugoslav and Serbian art critic Oto Bihalji-Merin.

black-and-white photogravures, were only one step towards the type of finely illustrated books that Lane had in mind. As W. E. Williams (1956, p. 15), Penguin's Editor-in-Chief and prominent adult educator, later acknowledged: 'Pelicans proved the basis of a vertebrate structure of creative publishing which was soon to include such other species as King Penguins, Puffins, Penguin Modern Painters, and [...] many other series.'

An ambitious attempt to enter the field of illustrated books came with The Penguin Illustrated Classics, a series modelled after the type of expensive and exclusive illustrated hardbacks published by The Bodley Head. The intention was to produce a paperback series with original wood-engravings comparable in quality but priced for the Penguin market. Ten titles appeared in May 1938, including *Pride and Prejudice*, *A Sentimental Journey*, and *Robinson Crusoe* with illustrations from members of the Society of Wood-Engravers. They were, however, unsuccessful. As Morpurgo (1979, p. 143) observed, 'the choice of title was almost too obvious; their newly created British audience expected from Penguin something more original than Jane Austen, Sterne and Defoe'. Furthermore, to the modern eye, the wood engravings appeared antiquated, 'as if they had been prepared by tired disciples of the old John Lane school of book illustrators'. Though exquisitely executed, the illustrations simply did not match either the youthful energy of Lane's firm or the small Penguin format, which caused them to appear cramped on the page. Furthermore, the cheap, thin paper used for the books meant that they could not compare with the sophisticated products they were attempting to emulate. Labelled a disaster, the series was discontinued after the first ten volumes.

Lane remained committed to pursuing illustrated books for the mass market and soon began to explore the potential of colour reproduction, an aspect of The Penguin Modern Painters that was routinely praised. In the 1930s, colour printing was well established as a technical process and, from 1937, was exploited to great effect in Britain by the firm Adprint. Founded by the Austrian émigré publisher Wolfgang Foges, Adprint specialised in producing greetings cards, commercial advertising and, with the assistance of Walter Neurath, illustrated books.[38] Foges, like Lane, wished to produce

---

[38] Walter Neurath had previously published illustrated books in his native Vienna. Fleeing Nazi Germany, he arrived in London in 1938, where he worked with

colour illustrated books that were both high-quality and affordable. Having witnessed the remarkable success of Penguin, Foges, and Neurath approached Lane proposing that they collaborate on a series of small reference books with colour illustrations. Lane was keen to work with Adprint in order to take advantage of Neurath's experiences with colour printing. Their collaboration resulted in The King Penguins series, which was launched in November 1939.

The appearance of The King Penguins coincided with the start of the Second World War, which led Penguin to market the books accordingly, promoting them in light of the recent closures of traditional art venues, many of which had been evacuated in anticipation of aerial bombardment. As Penguin's promotional publication *Penguins Progress* stated: 'At this time when so many of our galleries and museums are closed we hope [The King Penguins] will fill a useful purpose in promoting an appreciation of art and as a reminder of the pursuits of peace' (Penguin Books, 1940, p. 2). The early volumes were edited by Elizabeth Senior of the British Museum, but after she was killed in an air-raid in 1941 the series was taken over by Nikolaus Pevsner, an art historian and émigré from Germany. Pevsner had previously been commissioned to produce a King Penguin on the subject of illuminated manuscripts but had pulled out after seeing the poor quality of the colour reproductions. Despite Adprint's involvement, the illustrations of the earliest titles left much to be desired, reflecting the difficulties faced by Foges and Neurath who struggled to convey their exacting standards to British printers. As Morpurgo (1979, p. 144) noted, The King Penguins 'made demands upon the printer that seemed superhuman' as they were expected to 'somehow use mass-production to provide for the public a fair reconstruction of some of the most expensive and esoteric colour printing of the past'. An unimpressed John Piper (quoted in Carney, 1995, p. 49) remarked that the colours in the first books appeared to him like 'a mess on the bathroom linoleum'.

Lane was not discouraged, however, and improvements in printing came in 1942 when he hired R. B. Fishenden, a recognised authority on colour

Foges as production director of Adprint. Neurath later co-founded the publishing house Thames & Hudson with his wife Eva Neurath in 1949.

printing who would eventually oversee production of The Penguin Modern Painters. Under his expert guidance, the quality of The King Penguins improved significantly with colour plates executed using a variety of techniques such as halftone letterpress, photolithography and autolithography (Lake, 2014, p. 14). Though not selling in vast quantities, the enhanced books were very well received. Piper (1943, p. 104) noted that 'the pictures are distinctly better than usual', while Eric Newton (1949, p. 58) later praised the series for its 'balance between text and illustration which suggests neither a copiously illustrated essay nor a picture book with an artificial ballast of text'.

The war did not dampen Lane's desire to pursue illustrated books. If anything, it accelerated his resolve, providing him with the catalyst for the aforementioned Puffin Picture Books. The success of these and The King Penguins proved to Lane that not only was his firm capable of producing high-quality illustrated publications but that this could be achieved even during wartime. Lane's enthusiasm for colour illustrations, his confidence in Penguin's abilities, and the unprecedented public interest in art all gives the impression that The Penguin Modern Painters was something of an inevitability. However, there is little evidence to suggest that Lane had much personal interest in the work of contemporary British artists. Indeed, writing about the publisher after his death, W. E. Williams (1970) noted, rather disparagingly, that he had 'no interest whatever in art, music, theatre, science or politics. His tastes were unsophisticated and he showed no particular bent'. Did the Modern Painters simply reflect Lane's desire to capitalise on an emerging opportunity? Or was there more to the series than Penguin's profit and loss account? We now turn to consider another, possibly decisive factor, in Lane's decision to pursue The Penguin Modern Painters: the influence of W. E. Williams.

2.5 W. E. Williams: Editor-in-Chief

As Peter Mandler (2019, p. 240) has written, during the economic slump of the 1930s, Lane's 'mild social conscience' was pricked and he 'was quickly swept up into a giddy whirl of earnest social reformers and adult-educators'. Paramount among these was W. E. Williams who, as *The Times* (1977)

Art Books for the People

declared, could have claimed 'to have been one of the greatest and most effective mass educators of his time'. Williams believed in the self-empowering potential of reading and was keen to increase access to published materials, especially among the working classes. As Rick Rylance (2005, p. 60) observes, he 'favoured a unitary, inclusive definition of culture and a conception of the "public sphere" of books that embraced some painstaking attention to questions of access and use'. Williams began working with Penguin as an editorial adviser in 1936 and so confident was Lane in his abilities that he was soon promoted to Editor-in-Chief. As his biographer, Sander Meredeen (2008, p. 87), writes:

> In addition to offering meticulously detailed advice on particular books and manuscripts, Williams sustained Lane with sound strategic advice on the development of Penguin Books over thirty years, sharing ideas on a broad range of business issues, from the appointment of key personnel to the opening up of new markets, and from introducing a new series of publications to avoiding costly entanglement in matters outside the profitable core publishing business.

Lane's tendency to rely on advisers such as Williams stemmed from an awareness of the limitations of his own literary and scholarly abilities. He nearly always heeded Williams's counsel, especially in areas where he himself lacked knowledge, such as the arts. For example, it was Williams who, after being appointed general editor of Pelican, quickly expanded the list to include books on the visual arts alongside those on history, science, and politics. Williams's influence over the direction of Penguin Books, particularly in the area of the arts, is discussed at length in the next section, but it is worth briefly considering here the role that he played in the conception of The Penguin Modern Painters, especially with regard to the involvement of Kenneth Clark.

Indeed, Williams and Clark worked together closely during the war. Both were involved in CEMA and the Art for the People exhibitions, and Williams had briefly worked as Clark's personal assistant at the MoI. They both shared an interest in increasing the popular understanding of the arts, though it was Williams who understood the vast potential reach of Penguin Books. As the Penguin Archive reveals, it was Lane's Editor-in-Chief who steered the publisher towards Clark and possibly even planted the idea of publishing books on modern British artists – as opposed to books on war art exclusively – in his mind. This can be inferred from a missive from Lane to Clark in June 1942, in which the concept for the Modern Painters series was laid out: 'while discussing this [proposal] recently with Mr. Williams he suggested that I might get in touch with you and, if possible, arrange a meeting when we could talk it over' (Lane, 1942a). Could it be that Williams capitalised on Lane's previous dealings with Clark to ensure the involvement of his influential friend? Williams, as Lane's trusted advisor, certainly knew that a suggestion to approach Britain's most influential art world figure would be heeded. A further hint of Williams's progenitorial role is found in a letter he received from Clark written soon after he met with Lane: 'Allen Lane [has] been to see me about the Penguin "Modern Painters" and we have drawn up a promising looking list' (Clark, 1942b). Clark's use of the series title before it had been decided upon is intriguing, especially because Lane (1942b) was at this time referring to the project as the 'Penguin Modern Artist series'. Had Williams and Clark already discussed the concept for the series before it was suggested to Lane? Would Lane ever have considered publishing contemporary art books were it not for the gentle guidance and encouragement of Williams? As the next section will show, Williams, who was keen to see Penguin publish more educational books on the visual arts, had stronger ideological reasons than Lane or even Clark as to why The Penguin Modern Painters should be produced.

2.6 A General Editor for The Penguin Modern Painters

Although it was Williams who recommended that Lane should consult Clark regarding the Modern Painters project, Lane needed little encouragement to involve such an eminent figure. Not only was Clark the most powerful figure in the British art world, he was also popular with the general public. Driven by the belief that everyone should have access to culture, he appeared regularly on the BBC Home Service and his support for Dame Myra Hess's hugely popular wartime concerts in the evacuated National

Gallery had won him popular acclaim, as had his introduction of the 'Picture of the Month' scheme, which saw a succession of old master paintings retrieved from wartime storage and exhibited at the gallery. To have Clark's name associated with Lane's proposed series would have been a huge boon to Penguin. Yet, as Chris Stephens and John-Paul Stonard (2014, p. 9) note, he was also a contradictory character, appearing to some 'aloof and condescending, a man from the higher echelons of British society who managed to occupy the uncomfortable area where the establishment meets the artistic community'.

After meeting with Lane in London on 11 June 1942, Clark recommended that the most appropriate editor for the series would be Eric Newton, art critic of the *Manchester Guardian* and *Sunday Times* (Clark, 1942b). Newton was a prolific art writer, articulate lecturer, and radio broadcaster. His book *European Painting and Sculpture* had been published as a Pelican Special the previous year, and so he already enjoyed a working relationship with Penguin. Nevertheless, the opportunity to preside over a flagship series on modern British art for one of the country's most successful publishers proved too tempting for Clark and he hastily wrote to Lane the next day informing him that, in fact, he would rather edit the series himself (Clark, 1942c). Lane was naturally delighted and no doubt relieved, tactfully remarking that it was something he had not wanted to suggest himself as he knew how many calls there already were on Clark's time (Lane, 1942b).

As general editor of the Modern Painters, Clark was given free reign in selecting artists and authors for the series and while this represented a tremendous opportunity to advance the work of artists he personally supported, it also left him vulnerable to criticism. Fear of dissent perhaps lies behind his initial doubts about taking on the editorship: 'I should love doing it', he wrote to W. E. Williams, 'but of course my name is a red flag to a number of people in the art world' (Clark, 1942b). The art historian Herbert Read was one of Clark's most vociferous critics, judging him to be a dictatorial figure who promoted a narrow version of modernism and balked at abstract and non-objective art. Clark's anxiety over such criticisms can be detected in his comments to Lane suggesting reasons *not* to hire him: 'you may feel that my editorship would give the series too much of a *parti pris*', he wrote, 'or you may feel that I could not give enough time to it and you would rather have an editor whom you could hustle' (Clark, 1942c). Despite accepting the job as editor, his ambivalence became even more pronounced when a few weeks later he requested that his name not appear anywhere on the books: 'no-one ever notices who edits a series – at least I never do – and consequently no-one will observe that the editor's name has been omitted', he wrote to Penguin (Clark, 1942d). Clark's dubious reasoning did not convince Lane who recognised that his name was far too valuable to be omitted.

As soon as Lane had secured his editor, the new series, tentatively named Penguin Modern Artists, began to progress rapidly. Clark quickly compiled a list of artists whom he wanted to include, pairing each one with an appropriate author. Lane had decided that each author should receive £50, while the artists would be paid £100, but they were also expected to provide him with an artwork, free of charge, for his own collection. Initially, Clark left the choice of reproductions largely in the hands of the authors and artists whose judgement he trusted. However, in the case of authors who were 'primarily men of letters and not art critics', he ensured that the choice of images was left to himself (Clark, 1942f). This decision would prove problematic as several artists took issue with his selections, complaining that they should have been consulted first. Furthermore, in some instances, the precise location of artworks was unknown and, since Clark had little interest in detective work, the job of tracking them down fell to Penguin. In fact, Clark had very little involvement in the production of the Modern Painters, which was co-ordinated by Penguin's first in-house editor, Eunice Frost, whose role in the development of the series would prove significant. The Penguin Modern Painters – as Clark insisted the series be renamed, no doubt for its Ruskinian allusions – benefitted hugely from Frost's involvement. She undertook the majority of the editorial work and was also responsible for overseeing the physical production of the books under the most challenging of conditions. Her appreciation for art, sharp eye for detail and exacting standards all contributed to the early development of the series.[39] Clark's initial enthusiasm for the series began to wane after the war as various

---

[39] Before working for Penguin Frost had been Secretary of the Chelsea Arts Club. In later life she kept in regular contact with several of the artists featured in the Modern Painters series.

production problems were encountered, but it was here that Frost found herself in her element. She invested so much time and effort in the series that Clark regretted her role was not publicly acknowledged. As he wrote to Lane: 'the credit for [the books'] good qualities must go entirely to Miss Frost, who has put an immense amount of energy into them and has been wonderfully patient with the artists. I only wish that her name could appear as editor instead of mine' (Clark, 1944).

2.7 Overcoming Production Challenges

Frost's patience was tested time and time again while working on The Penguin Modern Painters and the Penguin Archive contains numerous examples of delays and setbacks. For example, when she wrote to the MoI's Publications Division, asking for permission to reproduce works from the WAAC's collection, she was told that her request would need to be put to OUP (Mont-Clar, 1943). This concerned Frost who was emphatic that 'in all cases the work has already been put in hand' (Frost, 1943a). The MoI, as has already been shown, were at times favourable towards Penguin, but in the case of the Modern Painters the planned series appears to have been considered something of a threat to its existing publishing activities. A determined Frost attempted to reason with OUP directly. 'It was not known to us that there was any ban in force against this and we very much hope that you will, in principle, agree to our reproducing certain of the pictures,' she wrote to Geoffrey Cumberlege (Frost, 1943b). Frost, having not received any word from OUP, was eventually contacted by Cecil Day-Lewis of the MoI who advised her that there would, in fact, be no difficulty in reproducing paintings by Nash, Sutherland, and Moore, but in the case of later titles, such as those on Bawden and Ardizzone that were to feature a larger proportion of war artists' pictures, 'Sir Kenneth Clark has agreed that it would be advisable to postpone their publication until the new O.U.P. Series has had its market' (Day-Lewis, 1943).[40] The Ministry clearly felt that Penguin's books would affect sales of the OUP series, and the revelation that Clark

[40] Penguin was required to pay the MoI a reproduction fee of ten shillings and sixpence per picture, even though it arranged and paid for its own photography.

was behind the delay must surely have irked Frost. However, in the event, the MoI need not have worried because, due to various other production challenges, the first Modern Painters books would not be ready for another year.

A significant delay was caused by Penguin's decision to have new photographs taken of each painting from which the reproductions would be produced. This meant that all of the works to be included in the Modern Painters needed to be located and photographed individually, either in situ or at the National Gallery's photographic department. Frost was responsible for tracking down the majority of the works, many of which were touring the provinces as part of WAAC exhibitions as well as those organised by the BIAE. Others, not belonging to the WAAC, institutions, or Clark and his associates, were harder to trace. Frost found herself writing individual letters to a host of private collectors in an attempt to ascertain the location of paintings, several of which had been sent abroad for safety and, in at least one case, the whereabouts of which was unknown. Finding the paintings, however, was only the first stage of the long and involved process of producing the reproductions for the books.

Creating accurate colour reproductions of paintings was, in the 1940s, a highly skilled and laborious affair. For the Modern Painters, Clark advised Lane to use the four-colour half-tone process, one of the more common reprographic methods of the day and the process employed by John Swain & Son and W. F. Sedgwick, Ltd., who produced the plates for the majority of The Penguin Modern Painters series.[41] But with this method, reproductions were at best approximations, the success of which depended largely on the interpretive skills of the photo-engraver and printer. The colour balance and contrast of paintings would frequently be rendered inaccurately in publications, resulting in images far removed from the originals. When, for example, Clark saw the illustrations accompanying an article about the war artists he had written for *The Studio*, he complained to the editor, saying: 'I am a little disappointed that the colour

---

[41] For a thorough explanation of the four-colour process and printing methods more generally during this period see Curwen (1947, pp. 114–18).

plates have improved so little since I saw the proofs. As usual they are too red' (Clark, 1941c).

The artist Paul Nash was well aware of the problems associated with colour reproduction. As he wrote in the 1936 *Penrose Annual*:

> [The artist] does not expect, if he is wise, to find his picture matched colour for colour; but he does require, for instance if his painting is cool, that he will be given the same temperature in the reproduction [...] Being a 'cold' painter I am particularly sensitive in this respect and I must confess that in all my experience I have never been spared the necessity of pointing out to the engraver that his print is too hot. (Nash, 1936, pp. 33–35)

The Penguin Modern Painters was no exception, and it took a long time before all the artists were satisfied with the proofs. As Nash's correspondence with Frost attests, the artist was indeed very concerned with the 'temperature' of the reproductions in his monograph. Numerous colour proofs were produced in an attempt to satiate him but rarely was he satisfied with the quality of John Swain & Son's work, which further delayed the progress of the first four books. Even after his monograph was published he still harboured reservations, writing to Lane: 'It is an excellent general effect but I am rather sad to find that by comparison [to the originals] the colour paintings ultimately lose their brilliance. Have I had a freak copy or was this inevitable?' (Nash, 1944a). However, in later correspondence, he conceded that he had probably overreacted, writing: 'I do not think I should have said I was disappointed with the final book, indeed I am very well pleased with it,' admitting that the differences between the reproductions and his original canvases were 'slighter than I thought' (Nash, 1944b). Despite this change of heart, Nash's ambivalence delayed the launch of the series by several months.[42]

Other volumes in the series did not fare so well. For instance, W.F. Sedgwick Ltd, the photo-engravers tasked with producing the images for

---

[42] The first four books, though published in April 1944, all carry the date 1943 and as such are frequently misdated by authors.

David Jones, was bombed during the war, and their blocks were destroyed. New blocks were not ready until 1947, but Jones, who was recovering from a nervous breakdown, was unable to provide feedback on them. When the book finally appeared in April 1949, Clark wrote promptly to Frost to complain about the poor quality of the colour plates:

> Thank you for sending the David Jones. It is, alas, a complete failure. If, when the series was first started, I had known as much about colour reproduction as I do now I should have realised that it was quite impossible to do a book on every artist. I am afraid it will do him nothing but disservice. (Clark, 1949)

The first four Modern Painters finally appeared in April 1944, a year after the second series of War Pictures by British Artists had been published (Clark's longed-for deluxe volume failed to materialise at all).[43] The arrival of the series was announced in *The Bookseller* (13 April 1944), where the books were commended for 'fully maintain[ing] the Penguin reputation for value for money' and subsequently selected as 'Publications of the Week' (20 April 1944). John Russell (1944, p. 526), writing in *The Listener*, hailed the books 'a pleasure to possess', remarking that 'the plates have [...] a remarkable veracity, and perusal of them, no less than of the essays, excites in every case the wish to see new works by these painters'. In *The Times Literary Supplement*, Charles Marriott (1944) wrote positively about the books, enthusing that a great advantage of the series was 'that it will enable at a moderate cost people who have not the time or the opportunity to keep up with contemporary art exhibitions to see for themselves what other people are making all the fuss about'.

Paul Nash (1944c) contacted Kenneth Clark to express his appreciation. 'Apart from being a very interesting gallery of pictures at an incomprehensible

---

[43] The WAAC instead focussed its energies on working with the publisher John Murray to produce Eric Newton's *War through Artists' Eyes: Paintings and Drawings by British War Artists*, a book that was not completed until 1945 when the war was almost over and demand for war-themed publications was quickly evaporating.

price', he wrote, 'it is a far reaching blow for the artist and the people at one and the same time'. Recognising the innovative nature of the affordable paperbacks, Nash saw their potential in introducing his work, and that of his peers, to a mass audience. His use of the widely overused term 'the people' is noteworthy; it echoes the Art for the People exhibitions but, as with that scheme, the specific demographic in view here is rather nebulous. As Margaret Canovan (2005, p. 2) has commented, 'like other terms that have been much contested, "the people" carries an assortment of meanings, many of them incompatible with one another'. While the term resists easy definition, in a broad sense it simply refers to a section of a society that does not belong to an elite. In this, it is comparable to the term 'general reader' so beloved of Penguin in the post-war years.[44] The notion that The Penguin Modern Painters was embraced by a broad cross section of the reading public has been suggested by Peaker (2001, p. 10), who asserts that, 'in Penguin's hands the art book shed its class distinctions and reached out towards a new broader audience, which greeted it zealously'.

But is that actually the case? To what extent were class distinctions really eschewed by the series? Who comprised this new audience and how broad was it? It is, of course, extremely difficult to establish accurately the composition of any publisher's readership. Lane attempted it in 1946, when he commissioned a study on Penguin's readers from the social research organisation Mass-Observation, though, as we shall see, this offered no conclusive evidence regarding the Modern Painters. What *is* possible, however, is to identify the type of audience that Penguin anticipated reaching with the series. It is the nature of this imagined, or constructed readership that the next section seeks to establish, and the extent to which this was reflected by the books themselves.

---

[44] On this subject see Tether (2019).

3 Penguin and the People: Identifying an Audience for The Penguin Modern Painters

3.1 W. E. Williams and The New Social Consciousness

As we have seen, multiple factors influenced the conception of the Modern Painters, but there was no greater champion of the series than Penguin's Editor-in-Chief, W. E. Williams who, recognising its educational potential, was key to identifying its target market. Writing soon after the war in Penguin's in-house magazine *Penguins Progress*, Williams (1946, pp. 46–47) claimed that The Penguin Modern Painters had been 'designed to bring the work of painters to the wide public outside the art galleries: the public who have perhaps never ventured within because they doubted their ability to appreciate what they would see'. For writers, Williams reasoned, the printing press had brought their work to 'a vast new world outside the lecture room'. Similarly, for composers, the wireless has introduced their music to 'an ever-widening audience outside the concert hall'. But the painter, he opined, had only been able to reach the small minority of people with access to galleries and museums. 'The work of our modern painters has lacked this general appreciation', he concluded, 'for the simple reason that its very nature prevents it from being both available and accessible to all but a limited public'. It was this perceived lack of accessibility to contemporary art amongst a supposedly uncultured section of British society that Williams thought the series should redress. By looking at the relationship between Williams's role at Penguin and his multifarious activities in the field of adult education, one can begin to piece together a picture of the readership he envisaged.

Williams dedicated most of his life to promoting adult education and the democratisation of culture. His remarkable career began as English master at Leyton County High School in Essex. In 1928 he was appointed Staff Tutor in English Literature in the Extra-mural Department of the University of London, the first appointment of its kind. By the time he began working for Penguin as an editorial adviser in 1936, he was editor of *The Highway* (the journal of the Workers' Educational Association) and Secretary of the BIAE, a post he held from 1934 until 1940. During the

Second World War he established the Army Bureau of Current Affairs (ABCA), where he served as Director (1941–45) and was appointed Honorary Director of Art at CEMA (1940–42), where he organised numerous wartime exhibitions in association with Kenneth Clark. In later life, he served as Secretary-General of the Arts Council of Great Britain (1951–63) and also Secretary of the National Arts Collection Fund (1963–70). As a writer he was a regular contributor to the BBC's literary weekly *The Listener* and authored or co-authored more than twenty books. But it was as Editor-in-Chief at Penguin books from the late 1930s to 1965 that he had his greatest influence on the reading tastes of the public at large. As Meredeen (2008, p. 77), argues:

> Without Williams' consistently wise and dependable advice, and his acute literary judgement over thirty years, Lane would not have enjoyed his brilliant critical and commercial success with Penguin Books. Allen Lane invented Penguin Books but, in a very real sense, Williams was the man who made Penguin Books successful.

It was not only Lane who trusted in Williams's counsel, Clark also sought his advice. For instance, after Clark had offered to edit The Penguin Modern Painters he confessed to Williams that he was 'not sure this was wise', worrying that his name 'might prejudice the sale of the books in some quarters' (Clark, 1942g). He continued: 'I am seeing Allen Lane about it on Thursday, but will not decide anything definite until I hear from you.' Williams (1942), however, had no reservations regarding Clark's editorship, remarking that his choice of artists and authors would make the Modern Painters 'one of the best Penguin lines so far'. However, he questioned Clark's initial decision to include the artist Richard Eurich and wondered if Edward Ardizzone was too 'limited' a subject. Of the authors, he noted that he was 'a bit tired of Herbert Read' and urged Clark to consider writing the introductions to *Graham Sutherland* and *Henry Moore* himself. Clark, however, did not intend on authoring any of the books, though he did heed Williams's advice regarding Eurich who, like Ardizzone, was dropped from the series. But Clark was not willing to lose Read, whom he felt was the most suitable person to write about Paul Nash. That both Lane and Clark sought Williams's advice illustrates the level of influence he enjoyed, and though he did not sway all of Clark's decisions regarding the Modern Painters, his influence over the early development of the series was not inconsequential.

When The Penguin Modern Painters was conceived in 1942, Williams was leading the Art for the People scheme with CEMA, which gave form to his belief that everyone should have the opportunity to appreciate and enjoy the fine arts. This conviction derived from the communitarian values instilled by his Congregationalist upbringing as well as his formative years in Manchester, where he had discovered for himself the treasures of the city's municipal art gallery. Following the nineteenth-century critic Matthew Arnold, many in the Adult Education movement of the 1930s believed that the democratisation of culture could improve social cohesion and create a united community that transcended class divisions.[45] As Albert Mansbridge (1934), chairman of the BIAE, wrote: 'if an increasing number of people would [...] live freely in the spirit of adult education, then new power and new happiness would be the reward of the entire community'. Indeed, the 1930s was an important decade in the push toward a common culture in Britain and, in the service of social reform, progressives and adult educationalists increasingly devoted themselves to improving the tastes of the general public.[46] But, as Raymond Williams (1989, p. 164) has stressed, adult educators were not interested in propagandising, nor were they involved with the movement out of pity for the underprivileged; rather, they were driven by

> the process of building a social consciousness of an adequate kind, as they saw it, to meet new crises, the crises that were then defined as war and unemployment and Fascism but that in any case were seen as the crises of modern capitalist society.

---

[45] See Arnold (1869).

[46] D. L. LeMahieu (1988) argues that this was spurred on by the growing dominance of mass media: Cinema raised its creative standards, the previously socially aloof BBC broadened its appeal, and national newspapers and magazines modernised their layouts to cater for an increasingly visually literate readership.

W. E. Williams, who understood the role that the arts could play in this new 'social consciousness', had brought this democratising ideology to Penguin, recognising in the Modern Painters an opportunity to further his cultural vision in book form. As has been shown, during the war, Lane, Clark and Williams all believed in the existence of a ready audience for affordable art books, a potential readership who, though largely uneducated in such matters, ostensibly desired to learn more about modern art. It was an assumption based on several factors. Firstly, there was the great interest in visual art precipitated by the war, not only in London but across the country. With the Blitz had come the perception that culture was under threat, which sparked a general enthusiasm for art unseen before 1940. As John Rothenstein (1966, p. 42) recalled, there was during the war 'an unprecedented demand for opportunities of seeing works of art', which for him was 'a characteristic manifestation of the enhanced seriousness of the national temper'. This demand was not entirely surprising considering that the national art collections had been removed to safety and many venues remained closed for the duration of the war, but it contrasted sharply with the situation prior to the Blitz. Furthermore, Rothenstein notes that the 'new public' for art which emerged in that period was also hungry to learn, demanding 'instruction as well as delight'.

Secondly, there was the increased demand for books, which, as discussed in Section 2, had seen Penguin's sales rocket in 1941. Thirdly, there was the success of OUP's War Pictures by British Artists, of which a second series was being prepared for 1943. The war had thus presented Penguin with the ideal conditions in which to launch a series of accessible and affordable contemporary art monographs. With the security of sufficient paper stock, Lane was sure that the project would be financially viable, but Williams saw another opportunity, one that would allow him to continue using Penguin as a tool to encourage new audiences for art, a mission that had begun during his time as editor of Pelican Books. To that end, Williams (1946, p. 47) was keen to ensure that The Penguin Modern Painters was accessible, educational, and targeted at people who believed that 'modern painting is something unintelligible, and that modern Art Galleries are for the few, selected initiates'.

3.2 Pelican Books and the Arts

Williams's editorship of Penguin's non-fiction imprint, Pelican Books, set an important precedent for the development of the Modern Painters. As he later acknowledged, 'Pelicans proved the basis of a vertebrate structure of creative publishing which was soon to include [...] Penguin Modern Painters' (Williams, 1956, p. 15). Initially, Pelican Books was aimed at adult students enrolled on non-vocational courses, such as those run by the WEA and university extra-mural departments. But Williams, who believed that readers should be equipped with the tools by which they could form their own tastes and opinions, recognised that cheap paperbacks were an ideal way to reach those sections of society outside the influence of formal educational institutions. He thus sought to widen the appeal of Pelican Books, attaching the project to 'an optimistic reformist social agenda' aimed at a 'large, intelligent reading public' who were increasingly hungry for non-fiction books (Rylance, 2005, p. 56). Having superseded V. K. Krishna Menon as general editor of the list in 1938, Williams became central to the development of Pelican and the conception of its readership. Having recognised the educational advantages that Penguin's growth could engender, Williams sought to further align the publisher's activities with his own aspirations in the fields of literature and the arts. Thus Lane, with Williams's guidance, was able to transform the image of Penguin from supplier of cheap fiction to that of the nation's new *Popular Educator*.[47]

Williams believed that everyone was capable of enjoying the fine arts, provided they were given sufficient guidance, and for him Pelican represented a vehicle by which that guidance could be delivered. As Lane (1938, pp. 968–69) acknowledged, the Pelican list had initially been heavily weighted on the side of history, sociology, politics and economics. But in 1938, with Williams at the helm, he could promise readers that 'a whole series of books in every field of Art' was soon to be published. Williams was convinced that there was a much larger appetite for art among the general public than Lane had hitherto imagined, one that could

---

[47] John Cassell's *Popular Educator* was a successful Victorian periodical for autodidacts.

only grow if suitably encouraged. If this audience was to be properly nourished, it was essential that the new Pelicans were suitably appetising. Lane therefore proclaimed that the books would feature no 'highbrow art criticism' and would treat the subject of art *'as a human activity'*. In this way, the two men anticipated Pelican books becoming 'the true everyman's library of the twentieth century, covering the whole range of the Arts and Sciences, and bringing the finest products of modern thought and art to the people' (Williams, 1937, p. 974). The editorial shift, indicated by talk of accessibility and an appeal to 'the people', reflected a re-evaluation of Pelican's readership. Instead of being targeted primarily at adult education students, the books would now be aimed at the much wider, if less readily defined, category of the 'intelligent layman', a nebulous readership that 'was deemed to be at the centre of Penguin's democratic revolution' (Blackburn, 2020, p. 21).

3.3 Williams and the Adult Education Movement

Lane and Williams recognised that to successfully market educational books on the arts to a mass audience, elitism was to be avoided at all costs. The changes in editorial policy that Williams (1934a, p. 7) made at Penguin reflected his belief that the 'pedantry of academic exposition' had made certain subjects 'alien and unintelligible' to students enrolled in formal adult educational schemes such as the WEA's Tutorial Classes. These university-based courses, established by Albert Mansbridge in 1907, involved the provision of educational opportunities to working people who had left formal education at an early age. They were founded on the assumption that 'there were great numbers of working people perfectly capable of profiting by more advanced education, even of the university standard' (Williams, 1938b, p. 8).[48] Prior to the 1930s, adult education classes and courses were largely oriented towards the social sciences with little reference to the arts, but during the 1930s classes on aesthetic appreciation began appearing, fostering a growing interest in art and an increased demand for art education.

While the Second World War may have precipitated the emergence of a new public for art, a growing interest in the arts among adult students had

---

[48] On the WEA, see Fieldhouse (1996, pp. 166–98).

been observed some years earlier. As Mansbridge (1935, p. 1), now Chairman of the BIAE, noted:

> during recent years it has become more and more evident that the adult student is extending his range of interests. He is no longer, as he once was, exclusively preoccupied with the study of the social sciences; he is now equally striving for an understanding of literature, music and art.

Williams himself experimented with such classes in 1934 when he decided to introduce his English Literature students to modern art. Armed with printed reproductions of works by Van Gogh, Paul Nash and others, he began a class on aesthetic appreciation, which proved very successful.[49] Nevertheless, he worried that such classes risked alienating the 'unsophisticated' if they became overly academic (Williams, 1934a, p. 19). Many students wrote to him at *The Highway* bemoaning the lack of elementary level classes. He therefore encouraged the cultivation of new forms of adult education that would appeal to those intimidated by the formality of the WEA Tutorial Class.

Writing in *The Highway*, Williams (1934b) challenged his peers regarding the formality and overly intellectual nature of the adult education movement: 'we persistently talk over [the adult student's] head; we expect more intellectual agility from him than he can possibly have after many years of absence from formal intellectual exercise; we won't begin from his level'. For Williams it was imperative that facilities were provided 'not for a coterie but for a community', adding that 'we have to organise not for tens of thousands but for hundreds of thousands'. Adult education thus needed to 'learn the needs and the idiom of that elusive but ubiquitous creature, the man-in-the-street' (Williams 1938b, p. 18). Using the metaphor of a swimming pool, Williams (1934a, p. 7) encouraged his adult education colleagues to cater for this expanded community of adult learners, reminding them that there was a 'shallow end' as well as a 'deep end':

> We stand by and watch the novice plunging out of his depth, and we even encourage him in such hazardous behaviour.

---

[49] See Williams (1934a, p .7).

> Most of those with whom we have to deal are shallow-enders. The ten-foot-enders and the high divers must have all the room and all the apparatus they need; but they will always be a minority. Meanwhile there are in the modern community vast numbers of spectators who are reluctant even to paddle. The most immediate and pressing need in adult education is to turn the spectators into shallow-enders.

Williams increasingly advocated an informal approach to adult learning, one that was less 'intellectually arduous' and that allowed more people to become participants rather than spectators. Bringing this perspective to Penguin, he had convinced Lane that it was the novice – the reader who needed to be tempted into the 'shallow-end' – that they should be targeting with Pelicans. It was an attractive proposition to Lane, for an expanded market would certainly result in increased sales.

3.4 Pelicans and the 'Man in the Street'

In October 1938, there appeared on the Pelican list a book on art aimed firmly at the 'man in the street'. Prompted by the centenary of John Constable's death, *Art in England* comprised a selection of essays compiled by R. S. Lambert (1938, p. 5), editor of *The Listener*, that was intended to provide an 'accessible and up-to-date book on art in [England] for the general reader'. Lambert hoped that the collection would 'meet the needs of that large and increasing section of the public which is becoming more and more interested in the visual arts and perhaps, at the same time, more and more puzzled about their present development'. Lambert was a former WEA tutor and had edited *The Highway* before Williams. As vice-chairman of the BIAE, he was one of Williams's closest allies and collaborators in the Adult Education movement. He was similarly interested in popularising the arts and was convinced of the necessity of 'bridging the gulf between the highbrow and the man in the street in matters of entertainment and culture'.[50]

---

[50] 'R. S. Lambert', biographical notes inserted into copies of *Art in England* (1938).

A growing public interest in art during the 1930s had been noted by several commentators, including W. G. Constable (1935), Director of the Courtauld Institute, who remarked:

> people are interested as never before in our days, in matters of art. They are anxious to learn its alphabet; they are ready to consider experimental work; they are curious about the methods and intentions of painters, designers, sculptors and architects.

The essays in *Art in England*, all of which were reproduced from *The Listener*, were written by various contributors, including Eric Newton, Herbert Read, Henry Moore, William Coldstream, Kenneth Clark, and W. E. Williams. Williams's belief that there was an 'appetite for art' among Britain's book-buying public was vindicated by the popularity of *Art in England*, which by October 1938 had rapidly become one of the best-selling Pelicans. By January 1939, over half of its initial impression had been sold which, as a member of Penguin's Publicity Department remarked was 'very good for a Pelican title' (Schurr, 1939).

Several of the essays in *Art in England* were first delivered as BBC radio broadcasts. The national broadcaster had been airing programmes on art appreciation throughout the 1930s, presented by figures such as Stanley Casson, J. E. Barton, and Eric Newton. As Rylance (2005, p. 57) has observed, to Williams 'Penguin was in many respects comparable to the BBC' and he was evidently in sympathy with its radio art talks, which, as Sam Rose (2013, p. 608) notes, were firmly aimed at the 'plain man' and sought to 'encourage a moderate and charitable attitude towards modern art'. They also encouraged listeners to visit the nation's art galleries, several of which organised exhibitions illustrating specific talks. As noted by S. F. Markham (1938, p. 137) in his report on the state of Britain's provincial museums and art galleries, at least two galleries installed loudspeakers in 1932 to enable visitors to listen to the talks in tandem with viewing the related exhibits. But whilst the BBC was reaching enormous numbers, access to art galleries was still limited. According to Markham there were only eighty public art galleries outside of London in 1938, and although many museums owned fine collections of art, these were confined to larger towns and cities. Like Williams, he believed that access to art had a role to play in societal improvement but warned that inadequate art education risked a cultural divide: 'on the one hand we have the narrow world of scientific attainment, refined scholarship, and trained aesthetic taste; on the other vast crowds whose art is dictated by the chain store, the cinema hoarding, and the seaside souvenir shop' (Markham, 1938, p. 143).

The notion that public taste needed to be improved was a common theme in the 1930s. For instance, Clark (1939a) noted that 'the English people have a fine taste in literature, but I do not think their best friends could claim that they have much natural taste in the arts of painting and sculpture'. His reasoning for the poor taste in visual arts among the English was attributed to the fact that, despite being subjected to 'good literature' from childhood, their walls are filled with 'very bad pictures, coloured supplements from winter annuals or steel engravings of highland cattle'. Similar views were expressed by Thomas Bodkin (1940), who at the start of the war noted that 'the Fine Arts are distrusted by the average Englishman because their value as helps to a full life are not appreciated [...] they are disregarded as being futile distractions from his two main preoccupations, business and sport'. Williams (1935, p. 141) reasoned that 'if popular taste is poor and ill-educated it is because it so seldom gets a chance to contemplate the examples of art which might illuminate its darkness'. As Secretary of the BIAE, he believed he could supply a remedy, and, in 1934, he began to devise Art for the People, a scheme that provides the clearest indication of the kind of audience that he was interested in stimulating.

3.5 Art for the People

Beginning in April 1935, Art for the People comprised a series of free touring exhibitions intended to compensate for the lack of municipal art galleries in the provinces. Williams (1937, p. 974) had calculated that there were more than four hundred towns with populations of over five thousand people in which there were no public art collections, and, according to the BIAE, many of these places were 'too small or too poor ever to possess a gallery of their own', thus it was not a case of 'bringing the people to art' but of bringing 'art to the people' (British Institute of Adult Education,

1935, pp. 7, 9). Williams's proposal soon found favour with his BIAE colleagues who agreed to administer the scheme with support from the WEA, the Carnegie UK Trust and a number of private donors. The first exhibitions were planned by Williams (1935, p. 141) with the BIAE's Art Committee, and while Art for the People became a highly successful venture that continued into the war years, it was initially conceived as a simple experiment to discover how much local interest could be stimulated by 'exposing' people 'to the novel experience of looking at good pictures'.[51]

The first three exhibitions were held in towns with significant working-class populations: Swindon, Barnsley, and Silver End in Essex. It was, of course, the working classes at whom much adult education was aimed but, in choosing these locations, it is clear that Williams and the BIAE intentionally targeted this section of society. The choice of venues reflected the organisation's desire to 'strike a balance between industrial and rural populations' (British Institute of Adult Education, 1935, p. 11). These were also places where adult education initiatives were already present. Swindon and Silver End, for example, both had active local branches of the WEA, which were able to assist in publicity and encourage participation. All three exhibitions were an emphatic success with the total number of adult visitors across the venues exceeding ten thousand.[52]

Crucial to the scheme's success was the securing of artworks. Legal restrictions at the time meant that loans from public collections were only available to accredited galleries and so, unable to secure pictures from national or regional art collections, the BIAE managed to persuade several private collectors to lend works to the exhibitions. With the exception of a couple of loans from the Contemporary Art Society and Courtauld Institute, the included artworks, all of which were paintings and drawings, were sourced from private collections. For example, the historian and educationalist Michael Sadler, himself a former resident of Barnsley, lent

---

[51] The BIAE's Art Committee was chaired by W. G. Constable and comprised W. E. Williams, R. S. Lambert, R. A. Rendall (a regional BBC Programme Director), Dr. Jane Walker and S. Myers (BIAE).

[52] In addition to adults, five thousand school children saw the three exhibitions in total. For visitor figures see British Institute of Adult Education (1935, p. 18).

his entire collection of English and French Impressionist and Post-Impressionist paintings to the South Yorkshire town's exhibition. Among the many British artists included in these first three shows, it is noteworthy that a large percentage were also selected for inclusion in The Penguin Modern Painters. Artists such as Duncan Grant, Ivon Hitchens, William Nicholson, Matthew Smith, Stanley Spencer, Paul Nash, David Jones, and Ben Nicholson were exhibited alongside Boudin, Cézanne, Gauguin, Daumier, Matisse, Pissarro, and Van Gogh.

The choice of artworks at these exhibitions was designed to introduce modern art to new audiences and thereby improve public appreciation for such work. Williams (1935, p. 142) was keen to note that the exhibitions were not designed to 'foist an artificial sense of "good taste" upon people, but to give them some opportunity to gain the experience on which they may ultimately come to base their conceptions of art'. As Meredeen (2008, p. 67) has observed, Williams's intention was 'to stimulate the habit of looking at painting and sculpture and so develop more critical faculties amongst viewers'. Williams's use of the term 'the people' evokes the type of generalisations about the working classes that were made by Victorian social reformers. Indeed, parallels between Art for the People and the philanthropic exhibitions in the deprived East End of London organised by Samuel and Henrietta Barnett in the late nineteenth century were openly embraced by the BIAE. The Institute's report on the scheme noted that the Barnett's motivations were 'at most points similar' to their own, but whereas their Whitechapel exhibitions had been designed to inspire the establishment of art galleries, Art for the People was primarily intended to 'serve the centres where galleries are unlikely ever to exist' (British Institute of Adult Education, 1935, p. 9). Having seemingly taken on the Barnetts' mantle, Williams hoped that his scheme would engender a greater understanding and appreciation of art for the sake of class relations.

One of the most significant parallels between the Barnetts' exhibitions and Art for the People was the inclusion of 'guide lecturers' whose job was to answer visitors' questions and to initiate informal discussions about the artworks. The Barnetts' exhibition guides were described by *The Times* (26 March, 1883) as 'kindly educated folk [. . .] who explain the pictures to willing groups of listeners'. The BIAE's guide lecturers, or 'observers' as they were also known, were in turn described as a kind of 'super-steward' who functioned as 'animated catalogues' (British Institute of Adult Education, 1935, p. 10). Their main purpose was to 'keep an eye on people who were puzzled or who seemed at a loss about how to look at the pictures'. As one exhibition catalogue stated, the guide lecturers 'are ready to discuss how to look at pictures and to help visitors get pleasure from what they see on the walls'.[53]

For Williams (1938a, pp. 115–16), it was the 'tactful and friendly' observers at Art for the People exhibitions who 'have proved far and away the most useful way of helping people to get the best out of the pictures'. His description of their role provides an insight into his conception of the target audience for Art for the People:

> If they hear a blunt Yorkshireman say to his wife as he turns abruptly away from a picture: "Well, that's not *my* idea of a cherry-tree" – or whatever it is – it is the observer's job to barge in, in a casual way, and start an argument. It isn't his job to contradict – you don't enlighten anyone that way. It is his job merely to persuade the sceptic to explain himself more freely. If you can coax people to be more expansive about why they like or dislike something, you can often enlarge their understanding.

Here, then, is Williams's conception of the archetypal 'man in the street': a sceptical 'blunt Yorkshireman' with little knowledge of art, the very type of working-class person that would likely have been found in Barnsley at the first of the Art for the People exhibitions.

In addition to the observers, the BIAE arranged informal talks on aesthetic appreciation that were delivered two or three times a week at each venue. These were loosely based on the BBC's art talks and were given by leading authorities such as Eric Newton, John Rothenstein, J. E. Barton,

[53] Introductory notes to the exhibition catalogue *3 British Artists: Henry Moore, John Piper, Graham Sutherland*, Leicester Museum and Art Gallery, 22 November–28 December 1941.

David Talbot-Rice, and Edward Halliday, several of whom had appeared on the BBC. Art historical content was kept to a minimum in favour of an emphasis on developing the critical faculties of those unfamiliar with looking at art. Despite the BIAE's claim that Art for the People was simply intended to provide opportunities for people in small towns to access good art, the presence of observers and lecturers underscored the pedagogical impulse that drove the scheme.

Williams's belief in the existence of a large potential audience for art and art education outside of the formal structures of the adult education movement was vindicated by the BIAE's report on the first Art for the People exhibitions:

> the three exhibitions can claim to have shown that there is a keen popular interest in painting: not an extensive one when it is compared with public attendance at cinemas or football matches; but, when compared with things of its own kind, such as going to repertory theatres or going to classes in adult education, a substantial one. (British Institute of Adult Education, 1935, p. 32)

In just under a month, the number of visitors attending these three provincial exhibitions exceeded by more than a quarter the total number of students attending WEA classes across the UK in a six-month period. Concluding that Art for the People was a viable project, the BIAE began work on expanding the scheme and many similar exhibitions were mounted in the following years.

3.6 Expanding Art for the People

The war years saw a major expansion of Art for the People. By 1939, the scheme had secured a powerful new patron in Williams's friend Dr Thomas Jones, secretary of independent educational charity the Pilgrim Trust and an ardent supporter of adult education.[54] Jones had

---

[54] The Pilgrim Trust was founded in 1930 by the American philanthropist Edward Harkness. In 1927, Thomas Jones created the Welsh further education college Coleg Harlech, which was closely associated with the WEA.

agreed to put up £25,000 and, a few weeks later, the Treasury had been persuaded to make available £50,000 for the creation in 1940 of the Committee (later Council) for the Encouragement of Music and the Arts in Wartime (CEMA). Not only did this mark the beginning of state funding of the arts in Britain but it paved the way for the creation of the Arts Council of Great Britain in 1945.[55] The role of CEMA, as their slogan 'the best for the most' indicated, was to deliver high-quality cultural activities to the general public. But, as Weight (1998, p. 157) has observed, it also signalled 'a specific determination by Britain's political elites to foster national culture using the organs of state'. CEMA became a useful tool for the government who not only believed that it would help bolster morale but, by nurturing popular taste, would also grow an awareness of the culture and heritage for which the nation was fighting. To this end CEMA was responsible for organising nationwide theatre tours, orchestral concerts, and exhibitions. Williams was appointed Honorary Director of Art for CEMA and Art for the People became its official provider of exhibitions.

Now that substantial funds were available, Williams was able to rapidly expand Art for the People. In 1940, under the joint direction of Williams and Clark, the exhibitions were toured by CEMA to eighty villages and towns attracting an estimated 300,000 people (Leventhal, 1990, p. 298). Work was now drawn from the WAAC's growing collection as well as the permanent holdings of the Tate Gallery and National Gallery. Exhibitions were presented in various venues including town halls, barrack rooms, canteens and factories. Commenting on the scheme, Clark (quoted in Mellor, 1990, p. 20) remarked that the wartime exhibitions provided 'the only practical means of bringing pictures to the people, especially workers, who would never have the leisure to see them'.

The following year, ninety-three venues hosted exhibitions, which included several large thematic shows. The total number of recorded attendances at the major exhibitions was 367,000 (Williams, 1971, p. 21). In 1942, 205 major exhibitions were organised, with 249 the following year. In 1944, the year that The Penguin Modern Painters was launched, there

---

[55] On this subject see Leventhal (1990).

Art Books for the People   57

were 126 major exhibitions. The exhibitions were by now reaching a broad audience, yet Williams still believed that the target demographic should be the working and lower middle classes. This was confirmed by an Art for the People exhibition pamphlet published in 1943 (quoted in Meredeen, 2008, p. 70) in which he wrote:

> By taking art to towns where there is little or no provision for any kind of leisure occupation a section of the public can be reached which has hitherto hardly been touched [. . .] the housekeeper, the shopkeeper, the clerk and the artisan, the docker and the heavy labourer, these as well as the small "intelligentsia" who inhabit the fringe of such work-a-day towns are the people whose reactions are being sought.

However, by the time these words were published, Williams had already surrendered the art directorship of CEMA to Philip James in order to concentrate on his role as Director of ABCA, a decision that would see him enjoy less influence over the direction of CEMA's visual arts policy as well as the development of The Penguin Modern Painters (Leventhal, 1990, p. 308).

3.7 Contradicting Williams

For Williams, The Penguin Modern Painters represented an opportunity to expand the wartime work of CEMA. Indeed, the similarities between the books and the Art for the People scheme have not gone unnoticed. Joicey (1995, p. 152), for instance, has observed that the series owed much to Williams's scheme, carrying forward the aesthetic evangelism of the 1930s into the post-war years. Carol Peaker (2001, p. 26) has similarly noted that Williams's proposal for the Modern Painters 'resembled Art for the People in book form'. Certainly it was claimed that both projects aimed to disseminate the work of artists to a broad public who were largely unfamiliar with modern art, and both were similarly driven by a pedagogical impulse. For instance, a parallel can be drawn between the books' introductory texts and the kinds of insights into an artist's work that one may have gained by attending the BIAE's art lectures, or even from having engaged with an official observer. Yet there are also significant differences. Most obvious is that viewing artworks in reproduction is very different to experiencing them as physical objects. As W. G. Constable (1934, p. 17) remarked at a BIAE conference, 'nothing, however, can replace direct contact with works of art themselves. It is one of a teacher's first duties to get his students to visit and revisit every kind of fine building, gallery, museum and exhibition'. Furthermore, the dialogical experience of interacting with an exhibition observer, or having the opportunity to question a visiting lecturer, was impossible to replicate in book form. This would prove to be a challenge for the authors of the Modern Painters who ostensibly had little notion of the audience they were writing for.

If The Penguin Modern Painters was to challenge and enlighten the views of those who believed modern painting to be 'unintelligible' and that art galleries were for 'selected initiates', it was essential that, as with Pelicans, the introductory texts should address the intended audience in a way that was both accessible and educational while avoiding condescension. However, as Holman (1993, pp. 76–77) has observed, in this regard the series was not consistent in its approach:

> The texts assume a more sophisticated readership, with a wide-ranging knowledge of literature and music, and an up-to-date awareness of debates in contemporary art. Such sentences as 'Think of Rowlandson or Stubbs' do not seem pertinent to people who have never ventured into a gallery, but rather to those whose accumulation of cultural capital is already quite substantial.

This suggests that not only were the authors not briefed about the intended readership, but that many lacked the experience of writing for such an audience. Holman's citation is taken from *Henry Moore* by Geoffrey Grigson, which was one of the first books in the series to be published in 1944. It appears amid a discussion of Moore's use of colour in his two-dimensional works: 'think of taffeta in Reynolds', Grigson (1944, p. 15) writes, 'or in Gainsborough. Think of colour in such poets as Mickle or

Chatterton'. He continues by making reference to the water-colours of Cotman and Turner, and to 'the open and shut weather of Constable'. While Grigson's allusions would not seem out of place in an art history book, or in an art periodical such as *The Studio*, they appear incongruous in a series purporting to cater for uninitiated readers.

Grigson was not the only writer whose text did not befit Williams's target audience. To a greater or lesser extent, all of the early volumes of the Modern Painters assume a level of knowledge and understanding contrary to that proposed by Williams. For example, Herbert Read (1944, p. 9), in his text for *Paul Nash*, observed formalist traits in the artist's work that tended 'towards certain simplifications and emphases of a geometrical nature which could only have their origins in the cubism of Picasso and Gris: perhaps also in the futurism of Boccioni and Severini'. One must concede that the likelihood of Williams's 'blunt Yorkshireman' being familiar with avant-garde art movements such as Cubism and Futurism is remote. Especially impenetrable to the general reader are portions of Edward Sackville-West's introduction to *Graham Sutherland*. Not only does he presuppose a familiarity with artists such as Palmer, Blake, and Turner, but also with poets and classical composers:

> Look at *Green Tree Form*, *Red Monolith*, *Folded Hills*, and then read their equivalents in Gerard Manley Hopkins, in Dylan Thomas and George Barker. Or listen if you prefer music, to Sibelius' *Tapiola*, in which Nature strikes to kill, or his *Sixth Symphony*, or the Finale of Bartok's *Second String Quartet*. All these works employ that double imagery which drove Rimbaud away from poetry altogether, lest it destroy him. (Sackville-West, 1944, p. 13)

Elsewhere are found obscure statements such as: 'Sutherland's harmonic progressions will seem in general as rugose as Beethoven's, to those accustomed to the blandness of most contemporary English *gammes*' (p. 9). Sackville-West's text, which at times borders on the esoteric, displays little evidence that the author intended to avoid what Williams (1946, p. 46) described as 'the over-coloured phrases that so often disturb the uninitiated catalogue-buyer'.

Even Eric Newton (1947, p. 5) makes assumptions regarding his readers' knowledge of art history when he writes in his introduction to *Stanley Spencer* that the artist's work 'is not to be approached in quite the normal way – the way in which one would approach, for example Bonnard and Sickert or Toulouse-Lautrec'. Elsewhere, he writes that Spencer can be compared to 'an imaginary painter of the Early Renaissance, a man endowed with a little of Masaccio's simple grandeur and some of Ghirlandaio's prosaic charm, mingled with his own native enthusiasm', and reference is also made to Giorgione, Botticelli and El Greco, artists unlikely to be overly familiar to readers unacquainted with art galleries (pp. 15, 8). To be fair to Newton, the majority of his text is written in a relatively accessible style with little technical vocabulary. A clear attempt to nurture an aesthetic appreciation of Spencer's work is apparent from lines such as: 'each picture is a statement of a particular message, an illustration of a specific idea in pictorial form. Miss the particular message – or, worse, misunderstand it – and you have lost at least half your means of enjoying his art' (p. 6). Nevertheless, as with the majority of writers who penned texts for the early Modern Painters, Newton's assumptions about his readers are at odds with the audience so clearly outlined by Williams.

An author more in sympathy with Williams was the critic Raymond Mortimer (1944, p. 14), who adopts an explanatory tone in his introduction to *Duncan Grant* while attempting to demystify modern art for his readers: 'It is now accepted that the principal function of a picture is not to give information about the visible world, but to express the imagination of the painter and to infect the spectator with his emotion'. Elsewhere, he writes casually, informing the reader that '[Roger Fry] and Clive Bell were, I fancy, the first English writers to cotton on to what is called "modern" painting [. . .] Post-Impressionism has been a temptation and a trap to many apprentice painters: to try to distort before you can present is like trying to dance before you can walk' (pp. 6–7). However, the majority of writers appear to have no awareness of an intended audience, which suggests that there was a distinct lack of editorial guidance from Williams and Clark. Similarly, Lane did not intervene and no attempt was made to discourage the 'highbrow art criticism' that he had previously sought to disown (Lane, 1938, p. 968).

How, then, do we account for the discrepancy between the content of The Penguin Modern Painters and the claims that Williams made regarding his target readership? It is not known how much advice, if any, he gave to Clark and Frost during the commissioning of individual books, and there is no evidence to suggest that he was involved in editing the texts. We must conclude, then, that Williams had no involvement in the production of the books. In fact, little evidence of his editorial labours at Penguin exists at all. As Lewis (2007, p. 88) observes, Williams

> was always, by his own volition, a semi-detached figure within Penguin, combining sound editorial advice with his work for the WEA, Unesco or the Arts Council. Temperamentally and by job definition, he was a man for the broad brushstroke, a delegator rather than a hands-on, nuts-and-bolts publisher: he and Lane would come up with the bright ideas, and it would be up to [Penguin editors] Eunice Frost and A.S.B. Glover to see them through in practice.

It is also worth noting the surprising fact that Williams, despite his senior role, was never actually employed by Penguin, working, as he described it, 'in a strictly extra-mural capacity and virtually for out-of-pocket expenses' (Williams quoted in Lewis, 2005, p. 118).

During the war, Williams's attention was diverted away from Penguin as he became more involved in his adult education work. Much of his time was taken up with ABCA – for which he sought to bring the principles of adult education to Britain's servicemen – and also CEMA where, in his capacity as Director of Art, he continued to organise the Art for the People exhibitions. But when John Maynard Keynes became chairman of CEMA in 1942, Williams began to grow frustrated. Keynes disliked Art for the People and made life progressively difficult for Williams by introducing an elitist, metropolitan bias to the Council's activities. 'C.E.M.A. is getting under my skin', Williams complained to Clark (7 September 1942, cited in Leventhal, 1990, n. 71). 'Try as I will, I can do nothing right for [Mary] Glasgow and [Philip] James, both of whom seem animated by the increasingly obvious determination to put the B.I.A.E. right out of C.E.M.A.'.[56] Williams's troubles at CEMA – a time when he was perhaps at his most distracted – coincided with the commissioning of The Penguin Modern Painters.

3.8 Clark's Audience and the Market for Art

Even though Clark had championed the Art for the People exhibitions and shown an interest in promoting art to a broad public, Williams was perhaps naive to assume that his own notion of a popular audience was shared by the general editor of The Penguin Modern Painters. Clark's interests lay primarily in supporting artists rather than the cultural edification of the working classes. His conception of a target audience for the Modern Painters was informed chiefly by his role as a patron. He certainly understood that the series was 'intended to attract people with little or no previous knowledge of modern painting' (Clark, 1942h), but as he later remarked, he had found editing the series valuable 'because it helped people to understand painters whose work they could buy, and it thereby helped the painters' (Clark, 1954). This comment highlights the diverging concerns of Williams and Clark: both men believed in educating the public about art, but whereas Williams longed for social change, Clark sought to support artists by cultivating patronage at a time when they needed it most.

Clark was well aware of the precarious position that artists found themselves in during the early months of the war. Unemployment rose sharply in the autumn of 1939, and a survey undertaken by the Artists' International Association between late September and early October discovered that 73 per cent of its members had either lost commissions or were out of work altogether (Morris and Radford, 1983, p. 56). The art market virtually collapsed during the first two months of the war. Brian Foss (2007, p. 10) notes that anxiety over air raids led several London dealers to suspend their activities, and, although other galleries lowered prices in order to stimulate sales, 'a long list of well-known figures from Stanley Spencer to Harold and Laura Knight and Frank Beresford found themselves in the unaccustomed position of having neither commissions nor sales'. Against

---

[56] Mary Glasgow was a civil servant, and CEMA's first secretary. Philip James had previously worked as keeper of the library of the Victoria and Albert Museum.

this background, Clive Bell (1939, p. 518) called for the government to step in and 'save the artists'. Keeping 'artists at work on any pretext' had been Clark's (1977, p. 22) rationale for establishing the WAAC, and, later, The Penguin Modern Painters represented a further opportunity for him to promote their work at a time when the market was beginning to recover.

From 1941, unemployment began to fall and personal income and savings rose substantially. According to Foss (2007, pp. 178–79), many first-time, middle-class buyers began to enter the market and exhibitions soon started selling out. As one columnist remarked, 'if interest, activity, and demand are criterions, then this is the golden age of British painters as surely as the Elizabethan era was the golden age of playwrights. Never has there been such a demand for pictures. Never were painters so profitably busy' (Edinger, 1943, p. 2). It was this group of enthusiastic new buyers whom Clark presumably wanted to target with The Penguin Modern Painters. Just as Allen Lane had perceived a market for art books, so Clark saw a large, untapped market for art. As Foss (2007, p. 173) has commented: 'Clark associated the fostering and popularising of artistic excellence with the reinstitution of a vigorous, enlightened system of patronage.' Indeed, the potential benefit of the Modern Painters to the art market was noted by art dealer Dudley Tooth, who wrote to Frost to express his support for the series, which he believed would boost the sales of works by contemporary British artists (Tooth, 1944). This may help explain why, in March 1946, after the war had ended and the market had recovered, Clark resigned from his role as general editor.[57]

Unlike Williams, Clark was not interested in countering the scepticism of those unfamiliar with modern art, and this was reflected by his choice of authors. Despite the fact that the books addressed a more sophisticated readership than envisaged by Penguin, Williams does not appear to have made any effort to make the texts more appealing to the 'man in the street', even though he maintained that the books were aimed specifically at this

---

[57] Lane (1946) was not prepared to forgo the advantages of Clark's association with the series; as he noted to Frost, 'it's not the amount of work he does which is important, but as you say, [his] is an extremely good name to have'. Despite his resignation, Clark's name continued to appear on the books until the early 1950s.

group. By the time Williams's comments about the series appeared in *Penguins Progress* two years had passed since the first four volumes of Modern Painters were published. By that time, each title had sold out and been reprinted. Volumes on Matthew Smith, John Piper, Edward Burra, and Victor Pasmore had also appeared, and though they sold well, it is doubtful that Williams's 'blunt Yorkshireman' had been responsible for their success. From Lane's perspective, high sales meant that there was no need to change anything about the series as it was clearly meeting a demand. But if the books were not being bought by the proverbial 'man in the street', who was buying them? While it is impossible to arrive at a conclusive answer to this question, a 1947 study into Penguin's readership provides evidence from which inferences can be drawn. It is that study and its findings to which we will now turn.

3.9 Mass-Observation and Penguin World

Although there is no evidence that Penguin issued any editorial guidance for The Penguin Modern Painters, the question of who constituted Penguin's readership evidently became a subject of intense interest to Lane and his editors which, as Blackburn (2020, p. 16) notes, 'led the publisher to question the idea that its audience was an anonymous mass whose qualities were indeterminate'. As Williams (1946, pp. 7–8) wrote in *Penguins Progress*: 'in these unreticent pages we tell you about ourselves; but what are *you* like?' he asked, continuing in his inimitable style:

> This, as any publisher will tell you, is no idle curiosity. Whenever publishers meet together, as they frequently do, one deep mystery absorbs their minds [. . .] they talk about the Reading Public, its veiled, bewitching lineaments, its unpredictable but delectable foibles, its maddening caprices, its enchanting favours. They are like a lover doting upon his true love. They are men bemused; the Reading Public, their Belle Dame Sans Merci, holds them in thrall.

The 'Penguin Public', as the firm's readers came to be known, were described by Marghanita Laski (1956) in the *Sunday Observer* as 'indefinable in terms of age or class or money or occupation or education'. The inability to define this group, it was claimed, was due to the fact that its members included readers from across virtually all sections of society. However, Laski's anecdotal description of Penguin's readership portrayed a distinctly middle-class audience, which stood opposed to Williams's notion of 'shallow enders' who needed coaxing into deeper waters. In her estimation, the Penguin Public were sophisticated autodidacts who tended 'to read *The Observer*, to listen to the Third Programme, use the public libraries, join the Film Society, go to concerts and art exhibitions, look critically at architecture and watch birds'.

Laski's conjecture found empirical support in a major study of Penguin's readership and general attitudes to its books undertaken by social research organisation Mass-Observation in 1946.[58] The study, commissioned by Lane, involved a thousand formal interviews of readers, retailers, wholesalers, and librarians, and sought to establish the identity of the Penguin Public. The results were presented to Lane in November 1947 in a document titled 'A Report on Penguin World'.[59] The study recorded that those who bought Penguin books constituted just 9 per cent of the British public (p. 31). In regard to the social make-up of this group, it concluded that 'middle class book readers are very much more likely to be Penguin readers than people from any other class group; slightly over five times as likely in fact, as the working class reader' (p. 32). In fact, the Penguin Public was found to be 'considerably more middle class than artisan or working class' (p. 33). Of the middle-class respondents, 41 per cent had read a Penguin book, compared with 17 per cent of artisan book readers and just 8 per cent of the working class (p. 32). The study noted that those who read Penguin books tended to

---

[58] Mass-Observation was a quasi-anthropological organisation whose purpose was to observe and record everyday life in Britain. Its investigators conducted interviews, surveyed behaviour at public events, kept diaries, and wrote reports. The organisation's work offers a rare source of information regarding popular attitudes and opinions in Britain between 1937 and 1949. See Hinton (2013).

[59] Several typescripts of *A Report on Penguin World* exist with differing pagination. All citations in this section are from the November 1947 version in the Penguin Archive: DM1843/14/1.

read more of everything, not just books but also newspapers and magazines, to a much greater degree than the ordinary public.

Of particular interest to Williams were the findings relating to Pelican. Whilst The Penguin Modern Painters was published as a part of the Penguin list, its content was more closely aligned with the aspirations of Pelican. It is worth noting here Morpurgo's (1979, p. 123) observation that 'the frontier between the two lists was not easy to define' and some subjects found their way into both 'for no reason, it seemed, beyond the whim of the moment'. Nevertheless, no books about art had appeared on the Penguin list prior to 1944, whereas several had appeared as Pelicans. It is reasonable, therefore, to surmise that the Penguin reader buying a volume from the Modern Painters series would more than likely have also taken an interest in Pelican titles. Mass-Observation calculated that, of the Penguin Public, the proportion reading Pelicans was roughly four times smaller than those reading Penguin books. Whilst Pelican readers consistently read Penguins of some sort, the reverse was seldom the case (p. 33). In what may have been a disappointment to Williams, it was found that the middle classes were the greatest readers of Pelican: 17 per cent compared to just 4 per cent of artisan readers and only 1 per cent of working-class readers. Mass-Observation concluded that those who read Penguins and Pelicans were a small offshoot of the wider book reading public. Furthermore, this group comprised proportionately more middle-class readers who were more highly educated and generally younger than the average reader (p. 34).

The Penguin World report also found that the Penguin Public were more likely to be members of cultural and intellectual organisations (p. 42–3). In a section dealing with the way that readers spent their leisure time, the study observed that 'the Penguin readers' interest in films and theatre and radio, in sports and outdoor activities, in visiting people and in miscellaneous ways of spending their spare time is more marked than it is among people as a whole' (p. 46). However, no mention is made of gallery-going, despite a table showing the results of favourite leisure time activities among respondents (p. 45). These include categories such as drinking, dancing, sports hobbies, reading, and going to films and shows. It is here that Mass-Observation explicitly distinguishes the Penguin Public from Williams's conception of the plain man, whereby it is claimed that 'a preference for drinking is the only sparetime interest which is almost equally popular with the Penguin reader and "the man in the street"' (p. 46).

From Mass-Observation's report, a picture of Penguin's readership emerged that contradicted the myth of universal appeal expressed by authors such as Arthur Calder-Marshall (1947, p. 26), who claimed that 'everybody finally bought Penguins'. Indeed, the evidence it presented, writes Blackburn (2020, p. 59), suggested that 'many of Penguin's readers were located within an emergent class of technocratic professionals' and that their ownership of Penguin books 'came to be understood as a symbol of their membership of this emergent social formation, which could not be located within orthodox categories of class'. However, as Mandler (2019, pp. 251–52) notes, the definition of the 'Penguin Public' presented by the study 'set the bar too high', for it only took into account respondents who spontaneously mentioned Penguin when questioned about their engagement with paperbacks. In actuality, he argues, the true 'Penguin Public' was likely closer to around a third of the book-reading public as opposed to 9 per cent. Furthermore, he writes, the report's definition of working-class readers 'set the bar too low' for it excluded those referred to as 'artisans' of whom a quarter bought Penguins. Nevertheless, when combined, the figures for the artisan and working-class groups are still far lower than those of the middle-class readers, a fact that, as we shall soon see, prompted Williams to undertake some serious soul-searching.

3.10 Williams's Disillusionment

The revelation that the demographic of Penguin's readership was in fact far narrower than had hitherto been supposed led to a shift in Williams's thinking. Instead of seeking to influence editorial policy, he ostensibly embraced the report's findings. This is evidenced by a 1949 letter to Lane prompted by the suggestion of a junior editor that Penguin might consider introductions to academic subjects that were more accessible than Pelicans. Williams (1949) insisted that 'the increase of the second-rate tends to diminish the market for the first-rate' and reminded Lane that Penguin's policy was 'to make a large number of readers reach upward until they get into the Pelican class. If an easier option were offered them, they might not reach so avidly'. Williams had become convinced of what he now assumed to be the limitations of Penguin's readership:

> I am not convinced that outside our present range of readership there is a large untapped reservoir of potential customers. I don't believe we have reached saturation point in Pelicans – indeed I think we may get double the size of that audience – but I don't believe that, beyond these confines, there is a large number of people who can be persuaded into buying a cheaper literary commodity. Their mental wants, if any, are satisfied by the lower class periodicals, and their social habit will not be coaxed towards 'serious pleasure' of any kind.

Clark's disillusion with the book-buying public was also observed in the post-war years when interest in the Modern Painters had waned considerably. For instance, when Frost suggested that the series might be expanded to include books on Matisse and Picasso, he responded: 'Whether there is really any point in introducing the people of South Shields, at this late hour, to Matisse and Picasso I am far from certain' (Clark, 1954). For Clark, these painters 'were the product of a highly sophisticated society and can never be genuinely popular, although people may buy them out of snobbishness and curiosity'. How many people bought Modern Painters books out of curiosity, or even snobbishness, is impossible to say, though we may assume that this accounted for at least some sales.

By the 1950s, it was clear that Penguin had come to 'epitomise the divide between the educated classes and the rest of society' (Joicey, 1995, p. 11). Williams's belief in Penguin as a vehicle for democratising culture was crumbling and he publicly conceded the limited appeal of its books in 1956: 'The Penguin market, despite its ten million sales, is not a mass market, and the firm never intends to seek a truly mass market' (Williams, 1956, p. 58). Alluding to the findings of the Mass-Observation report, he continued by explaining that '[Penguin's] books, especially outside crime and detection, are deliberately designed to appeal to a readership which probably does not exceed one-tenth of the population, and there must accordingly be a limit to the number of titles which can be economically offered to such a restricted audience'. Williams (1963, p. 11) maintained this position into the 1960s, writing in *New Society* that, although Penguin could lay claim to the title of popular educator, 'that does not in the least imply that Penguins are made for the masses'. Citing sales figures of eleven million for the previous year, he noted that 'even that big figure only means that one in five of our population buys a solitary Penguin a year. Penguins are made for a minority, but that minority (or most of it) is a reading élite'.

Conclusion

By placing The Penguin Modern Painters in its proper social, political, and cultural context, this Element has shown that not only was the series a significant innovation in British art book publishing, it was also part of a larger project of cultural democratisation that had begun in the 1930s. The series was not, as Kells (2015, p. 184) suggests, 'oddly timed'; rather, it was the very rational response of a highly successful publisher to an extraordinary cultural phenomenon. The Second World War provided the subject, market, and, indeed, the resources that allowed Penguin to embark on such an ambitious project.

In examining the pre-history of the series, it has been demonstrated that the conception of the Modern Painters is inextricably intertwined with the state-sponsored activities of the WAAC. However, despite Penguin's early negotiations with the MoI, the series was not part of the Ministry's clandestine Books and Pamphlets Programme and received no direct support from the British Government. Indeed, it was the WAAC's rejection of Penguin in favour of OUP that gave Lane the opportunity to devise a superior project that was distinct from the War Pictures by British Artists series and transcended its immediate wartime context. The unprecedented public interest in art, which had been stoked in no small part by the exhibitions of the WAAC and Art for the People, provided a ready market for Lane's series, while the unique position that Penguin found itself in during the war allowed it to exploit that market by creating a product of unrivalled quality and affordability. Whilst Lane's confidence in embarking on the series was characteristic of the publisher's entrepreneurial character and reflected his long-standing desire to produce high-quality illustrated books, it was the unique set of circumstances engendered by the war that created the perfect climate for the series to exist and thrive.

As we saw in Sections 1 and 2, the emergence of the Modern Painters cannot be attributed to a single person. The seed of the idea may have originated with Clark's committee but it was Penguin's Editor-in-Chief, W. E. Williams, who realised its educational potential and urged Lane to consider pursuing the series with Clark as editor. But it was the administrative excellence and extreme dedication of Eunice Frost that ensured

Art Books for the People

the project developed successfully from initial concept to finished product. For Lane, The Penguin Modern Painters was a savvy business opportunity and a chance to pursue his ambition for high-quality mass produced illustrated books. For Williams, it had the potential to improve social cohesion as part of a post-war common culture, and while Clark was not unsympathetic to Penguin's democratising mission, he saw the series primarily as a way of encouraging private patronage to support struggling artists in an uncertain financial climate. It was this multiplicity of conflicting agendas that led to the lack of a clearly defined editorial policy.

With its roots in the ideology of the adult education movement and the aims of British wartime cultural policy, The Penguin Modern Painters reflects the shifting attitudes of the nation's cultural elites to the way that modern art was presented to the general public in the 1940s. In attempting to identify the market that Penguin anticipated reaching with the books, this Element has shown that the target readership was defined from the outset by W. E. Williams who, before the war, had been certain that Penguin could be an effective tool of cultural dissemination. Williams (1946, pp. 46–47) had high aspirations for the Modern Painters, intending it to reach the sceptical 'man in the street' who in his mind was working class, uneducated in matters of art but nevertheless interested to learn more. Without his influence, it is doubtful whether Lane would have ever considered pursuing the project. Although Williams had introduced guide lecturers at the Art for the People exhibitions, the role of these 'super-stewards' who taught puzzled visitors how to appreciate paintings, was not replicated by the texts of the Modern Painters. Despite his insistence that the series was intended to reach 'the wide public outside the art galleries' who were unfamiliar with modern art, there was evidently no consensus as to the composition of that audience or how it should be addressed. Considering that Williams was immersed in the politics of the working classes, ostensibly viewing the Modern Painters as an extension of his adult education work, the lack of direction given to the authors is surprising and not easily explained.

The Penguin Modern Painters proved hugely successful during the war, and though the books sold relatively well, they represented only a small fraction of Penguin's overall sales. Hare asserts that the series 'changed the way a whole generation thought about modern art and artists'.[60] Yet, as Section 3 demonstrated, its audience was in fact quite limited. The Second World War provided a new urgency for the promotion of a common culture that many cultural elites felt would improve social cohesion, and, as Joicey (1995, p. 25) notes, the restricted cultural market of the mid-1940s created the impression that the public for Penguin's books on art, literature, politics, and science might form its foundations. However, by the end of the decade, it was clear that The Penguin Modern Painters, along with many other Penguin and Pelican titles, could only ever appeal to a minority. Indeed, the tone of the series was more suited to the cultured elite that Clark initially had in mind when he floated his idea of a luxury publication to the WAAC. The claim made by Lane that Pelicans would contain no 'highbrow art criticism' could not easily be made for the Modern Painters and Clark's commissioning of critics, poets, and intellectuals appeared to make no accommodation for Williams's intended audience. The growing disillusionment felt by Williams was reflected in his public and private statements in the post-war years when any notion of the series contributing to a new 'social consciousness' had evidently been abandoned.

The history of British art publishing in the twentieth century remains largely unwritten and substantial questions are yet to be addressed. For instance, what has been the legacy of The Penguin Modern Painters? How does its appearance relate to the expansion of art publishing in the mid-to-late twentieth century? In what ways were artists' reputations shaped by the series and, indeed, art publishing more broadly? The activities of publishing houses such as Phaidon Press, Lund Humphries, and Thames & Hudson are integral to this larger history and invite further inquiry. Even within the history of Penguin Books there is scope for further research. For example, the successful Pelican History of Art series (1953–1987) and its role in the popular dissemination of art history have yet to be analysed. Also, the short-lived Penguin New Art series (1970–1972), for which there is a large amount of extant editorial material, warrants further investigation.[61] What factors, for

---

[60] Hare, 'Introduction' in Peaker (2001, p. 8).
[61] Intriguingly, the Penguin New Art series uses the same catalogue numbering sequence as The Penguin Modern Painters, suggesting that Penguin saw the new series as a continuation of the first.

instance, led Penguin to return to art publishing at the end of the 1960s? And why was the series not more successful at a time when, as Linda Lloyd Jones (1985, pp. 83–84) notes, Penguin was selling more books than ever? In demonstrating the type of insights that the study of art book publishing can provide for historians of art, as well as scholars of other disciplines, it is hoped that this Element will stimulate further research into the intersection of art history and book history.

References

Primary Sources and Archival Material

Arnold, M. (1869). *Culture and Anarchy*. London: Smith, Elder.

Bell, C. (1939). A Ministry of Arts. *New Statesman and Nation*, 14 October, p. 518.

Bell, C. (1945). *Victor Pasmore*. Harmondsworth: Penguin.

Betjeman, J. (1943). *English Cities and Small Towns*. London: William Collins.

Bevan, R. A. (1940). *Letter from R. A. Bevan to Kenneth Clark*. 20 May. War Artist Archive: GP/46/10, Imperial War Museum, London.

Bodkin, T. (1940). Who Cares about Art? *The Listener*. 2 May, p. 875.

British Institute of Adult Education (1935). *Art for the People*. London: British Institute of Adult Education.

Checksfield, M. M. (1940). Propaganda in This War. *New Statesman and Nation*. 16 March, p. 367.

Clark, K. (1939a). Art for the People. *The Listener*. 23 November, p. 1000.

Clark, K. (1939b). The Artist in Wartime. *The Listener*. 26 October, p. 810.

Clark, K. (1940). *Letter from Kenneth Clark to Allen Lane*. 9 December. War Artist Archive: GP/46/36, Imperial War Museum, London.

Clark, K. (1941a). *Letter from Kenneth Clark to David N. Lawson*. 19 August. Kenneth Clark papers: TGA 8812/1/1/1/60, Tate Gallery Archive, London.

Clark, K. (1941b). *Letter from Kenneth Clark to Allen Lane*. 7 January. Kenneth Clark papers: TGA 8812/1/1/1/33, Tate Gallery Archive, London.

Clark, K. (1941c). *Letter from Kenneth Clark to Frank A. Mercer*. 17 December. Kenneth Clark papers, TGA 8812/1/1/10/363, Tate Gallery Archive, London.

Clark, K. (1942a). *Letter from Kenneth Clark to Allen Lane.* 6 June. Allen Lane files: DM1819/31, Penguin Archive, University of Bristol.

Clark, K. (1942b). *Letter from Kenneth Clark to W. E. Williams.* 16 June. Kenneth Clark papers: TGA 8812/1/1/14/233, Tate Gallery Archive, London.

Clark, K. (1942c). *Letter from Kenneth Clark to Allen Lane.* 12 June. Allen Lane files: DM1819/31, Penguin Archive, University of Bristol.

Clark, K. (1942d). *Letter from Kenneth Clark to Eunice Frost.* 20 July. Allen Lane files: DM1819/31, Penguin Archive, University of Bristol.

Clark, K. (1942e). *Letter from Kenneth Clark to Eunice Frost.* 10 August. Allen Lane files: DM1819/31, Penguin Archive, University of Bristol.

Clark, K. (1942f). *Letter from Kenneth Clark to Allen Lane.* 17 September. Allen Lane files: DM1819/31, Penguin Archive, University of Bristol.

Clark, K. (1942g). *Letter from Kenneth Clark to W. E. Williams.* 16 June. Kenneth Clark papers: TGA 8812/1/1/14/233, Tate Gallery Archive, London.

Clark, K. (1942h). *Letter from Kenneth Clark to Paul Nash.* 7 December. Paul Nash papers: TGA 7050/1036, Tate Gallery Archive, London.

Clark, K. (1944). *Letter from Kenneth Clark to Allen Lane.* 22 April. Eunice Frost papers: DM1843/8, Penguin Archive, University of Bristol.

Clark, K. (1949). *Letter from Kenneth Clark to Eunice Frost.* 11 April. Kenneth Clark papers: TGA 8812/1/4/331, Tate Gallery Archive, London.

Clark, K. (1954). *Letter from Kenneth Clark to Eunice Frost.* 22 January. Allen Lane files: DM1819/31, Penguin Archive, University of Bristol.

Clark, K. (1977). *The Other Half.* London: John Murray.

Constable, W. G. (1934). Art and Adult Education. *Adult Education*, 7(1), 8–17.

Constable, W. G. (1935). Art and the Ordinary Man. *The Listener*. 3 April, p. 555.

Curwen, H. (1947). *Processes of Graphic Reproduction in Printing*. London: Faber and Faber.

Dane, W. S. (1939). *Letter from William Surrey Dane to Ivison Stevenson Macadam*. 4 December. War Artist Archive: GP/46/10a, Imperial War Museum, London.

Dark, S. (1922). *The New Reading Public: A Lecture Delivered under the Auspices of 'The Society of Bookmen'*. London: Allen & Unwin.

Day-Lewis, C. (1943). *Letter from Cecil Day Lewis to Eunice Frost*. 28 April. Eunice Frost papers: DM1843/56, Penguin Archive, University of Bristol.

Dickey, E. M. O'R. (1939). *Letter from E. M. O'R. Dickey to the MoI's Deputy Director General*. 6 December. War Artist Archive: GP/46/10a, Imperial War Museum, London.

Dickey, E. M. O'R. (1940a). *Letter from E. M. O'R. Dickey to Secretary*. 11 December. War Artist Archive: GP/46/10, Imperial War Museum, London.

Dickey, E. M. O'R. (1940b). *Letter from E. M. O'R. Dickey to Kenneth Clark*. 1 October. War Artist Archive: GP/46/10a, Imperial War Museum, London.

Dickey, E. M. O'R. (1940c). *Letter from E. M. O'R. Dickey to H. R. Francis*. 28 November. War Artist Archive: GP/46/36, Imperial War Museum, London.

Dickey, E. M. O'R. (1940d). *Letter from E. M. O'R Dickey to Muirhead Bone*. 4 July. War Artist Archive: GP/72/D (1), Imperial War Museum, London.

Edinger, G. (1943). Everybody Wants to Buy a Picture. *Daily Mail*. 24 April, p. 2.

Fraser, R. (1941). *Books and Pamphlets Programme*. 4 December. Ministry of Information papers: INF/123, The National Archives, London.

Frost, E. (1943a). *Letter from Eunice Frost to Lona M. Mont-Clar*. 30 March. Eunice Frost papers: DM1843/56, Penguin Archive, University of Bristol.

Frost, E. (1943b). *Letter from Eunice Frost to Geoffrey Cumberlege*. 17 April. Eunice Frost papers: DM1843/56, Penguin Archive, University of Bristol.

Grigson, G. (1944). *Henry Moore*. Harmondsworth: Penguin.

Hancock, W. K., ed. (1951). *Statistical Digest of the War*. London: HMSO.

International Propaganda and Broadcasting Enquiry (1939). *Memorandum by the International Propaganda and Broadcasting Inquiry*. 21 June. Ministry of Information papers: INF 1/724, The National Archives, London.

Kitchin, D. (1938). A Revolution in Publishing. *Left Review*, 3(16), 970–72.

Lambert, R. S., ed. (1938). *Art in England*. Harmondsworth: Penguin.

Lane, A. (1938). Books for the Million . . .. *Left Review*, 3(16), 968–70.

Lane, A. (1940). *Letter from Allen Lane to Kenneth Clark*. 23 December. War Artist Archive: GP/46/36, Imperial War Museum, London.

Lane, A. (1942a). *Letter from Allen Lane to Kenneth Clark*. 3 June. Allen Lane files: DM1819/31, Penguin Archive, University of Bristol.

Lane, A. (1942b). Letter from Allen Lane to Kenneth Clark. 12 June. Allen Lane files: DM1819/31, Penguin Archive, University of Bristol.

Lane, A. (1946). *Letter from Allen Lane to Eunice Frost*. 25 April. Eunice Frost papers: DM1843/57, Penguin Archive, Bristol.

Laski, M. (1956). Penguin Public. *Sunday Observer*. 29 July, p. 8.

Lehmann, J. (1960). *I Am My Brother*. London: Longmans.

L. M. W. (1943). London Diary. *The Scotsman*. 8 March, p. 6.

Lewis, J. (2007). A Writer Responds. *Penguin Collectors' Society Newsletter*, 69, 88.

Macaulay, R. (1942). *Life among the English*. London: William Collins.

Manchester Guardian. (1945). 9 February 1945, p. 3.

Mansbridge, A. (1934). The Last Thirty Years in Adult Education, *Adult Education*, 7(2), 126.

Mansbridge, A. (1935). Preface. In British Institute of Adult Education. *Art for the People*. London: British Institute of Adult Education, p. 1.

Markham, S. F. (1938). *A Report on the Museums and Art Galleries of the British Isles (Other than the National Museums)*. Edinburgh: Carnegie United Kingdom Trust.

Marriott, C. (1944). Modern Painters. *The Times Literary Supplement*. 6 May, p. 224.

Mass-Observation (1947). *A Report on Penguin World*. Eunice Frost papers: DM1843/14/1, Penguin Archive, University of Bristol.

Milford, H. (1943). *Letter from Humphrey Milford to the Secretary, The Clarendon Press*. 8 October. Oxford University Press Archive: Sir Humphrey Milford's Letter Book 168, Oxford University Press, Oxford.

Ministry of Information (1939). *Co-ordinating and Co-ordination Committee Minutes*. 14 September. Ministry of Information papers: INF 1/867, The National Archives, London.

Ministry of Information (1940). *Commercial Distribution of Books and Pamphlets*. 23 December. Ministry of Information papers: INF/123, The National Archives, London.

Ministry of Information (1941). *Books and Pamphlets in Production or Planned*. 29 November. Ministry of Information papers: INF/123, The National Archives, London.

Ministry of National Service (1918). *Letter from Unknown Official to Alfred Yockney, Wellington House.* 21 January. First World War Artists Archive: G4010/27, Imperial War Museum, London.

Mont-Clar, L. M. (1943). *Letter from Lona M. Mont-Clar to Eunice Frost.* 5 April. Eunice Frost papers: DM1843/56, Penguin Archive, University of Bristol.

Mortimer, R. (1939). First Aid for the Artist. *New Statesman and Nation.* 29 July, p. 175.

Mortimer, R. (1944). *Duncan Grant.* Harmondsworth: Penguin.

Nash, P. (1936). Experiments in Colour Reproduction, with Some Observations on Modern Colour Prints. In R. B. Fishenden, ed., *Penrose Annual*, Vol. 38. London: Lund Humphries, pp. 33–35.

Nash, P. (1944a). *Letter from Paul Nash to Allen Lane.* 4 March. Allen Lane files: DM1819/31, Penguin Archive, University of Bristol.

Nash, P. (1944b). *Letter from Paul Nash to Allen Lane.* 19 March. Allen Lane files: DM1819/31, Penguin Archive, University of Bristol.

Nash, P. (1944c). *Letter from Paul Nash to Kenneth Clark.* 13 May. Kenneth Clark papers: TGA 8812/1/1/55, Tate Gallery Archive, London.

Newton, E. (1945). The Penguin Modern Painters. *Journal of the Royal Society of Arts*, 93(4687), 199–200.

Newton, E. (1947). *Stanley Spencer.* Harmondsworth: Penguin.

Newton, E. (1949). The King Penguin Books. In R. B. Fishenden, ed., *Penrose Annual*, Vol. 43. London: Lund Humphries, pp. 58–60.

Nicolson, B. (1946). Round the Exhibitions, *New Statesman and Nation.* 21 December, pp. 461–62.

North Devon Journal Herald (1942). *Art for the People.* 9 July, p. 2.

Out of Chaos. (1944). Film. Directed by Jill Craigie. London: Two Cities Films.

Parrish, M. J. (1940). *Letter from Max J. Parrish to R. A. Bevan*. 3 May. Ministry of Information papers: INF 1/238, The National Archives, London.

Penguin Books. *Sales Figures for Penguin Books 1935–1970*. Penguin Books, historical files: DM1294/4/2/7, Penguin Archive, University of Bristol.

Penguin Books (1940). Our War Aims. *Penguins Progress, First War Number*, p. 2.

Penguin Books (1944). *Press Release*. April. Allen Lane files: DM1819/31, Penguin Archive, University of Bristol.

Piper, J. (1942). *British Romantic Artists*. London: William Collins.

Piper, J. (1943). Colour Reproduction and the Cheap Book. *The Listener*. 22 July, p. 104.

Read, H. (1944). *Paul Nash*. Harmondsworth: Penguin.

Rothenstein, J. (1966). *The Tate Gallery*. London: Thames and Hudson.

Russell, J. (1944). Four Modern Painters. *The Listener*. 11 May, p. 526.

Sackville-West, E. (1944). *Graham Sutherland*. Harmondsworth: Penguin.

Sackville-West, E. (1955). *Graham Sutherland*. Harmondsworth: Penguin.

Schurr (1939). *Letter from Miss Schurr [Penguin] to Miss Morgan [The Listener]*. 6 January. Penguin editorial files: DM1107/02/0038, Penguin Archive, University of Bristol.

Somerset County Herald (1941). *Bringing Art to the People*. 5 April, p. 6.

Squire, J. (1942). *The Bookseller*. 1 October, p. 1.

The Bookseller (1944). *Penguin Modern Painters*. 13 April, pp. 355–56.

The Times (1977). *Sir William Emrys Williams*. 1 April, p. 16.

Thoene, P. (1938). *Modern German Art*. Harmondsworth: Penguin.

Tooth, D. W. (1944). *Letter from Dudley Tooth to Eunice Frost*. 15 April. Eunice Frost papers: DM1843/56, Penguin Archive, University of Bristol.

Unwin, S. (1941). The Bombed Book-Trade. *The Spectator*. 10 January, p. 33.

Unwin, S. (1944). *Publishing in Peace and War*. London: George Allen and Unwin.

WAAC (1939a). *Minutes of the Second Meeting of the War Artists' Advisory Committee*. 29 November. Registry files: Ministry of Information: Artists' Advisory Committee: NG16/120/1, National Gallery Archive, London.

WAAC (1939b). *Arrangements for the Employment of Artists to Record the War: Copyright and Reproduction*. 4 December. War Artist Archive: GP/46/10a, Imperial War Museum, London.

WAAC (1940a). *Minutes of the War Artists' Advisory Committee*. 14 February. War Artist Archive: GP/46/10a, Imperial War Museum, London.

WAAC (1940b). *Minutes of the War Artists' Advisory Committee*. 10 October. War Artist Archive: GP/72/D(1), Imperial War Museum, London.

WAAC (1940c). *Minutes of the War Artists' Advisory Committee*. 26 April. War Artist Archive: GP/46/10a, Imperial War Museum, London.

WAAC (1940d). *Second Interim Report. Paper No. 38 [draft]*. October. War Artist Archive: GP/72/D(1), Imperial War Museum, London.

WAAC (1940e). *Record of a Meeting between Mr. Allen Lane and Sir Kenneth Clark, 12.12.40*. War Artist Archive: GP/46/36, Imperial War Museum, London.

WAAC (1940f). *Minutes of the War Artists' Advisory Committee*. 5 December. War Artist Archive: GP/72/D(2), Imperial War Museum, London.

Williams, W. E. (1934a). *The Auxiliaries of Adult Education*. London: British Institute of Adult Education.

Williams, W. E. (1934b). Notes and Comments. *The Highway*, 26(4), p. 2.

Williams W. E. (1935). Notes and Comments. *The Highway*, 27(3), p. 141.

Williams, W. E. (1937). Art for the People. *The Listener*. 19 May, p. 974.

Williams, W. E. (1938a). Art for the People. In R. S. Lambert, ed., *Art in England*. Harmondsworth: Penguin, pp. 113–18.

Williams, W. E. (1938b). The Changing Map of Adult Education. In W. E. Williams, ed., *Adult Education in Great Britain and the United States of America*. London: British Institute for Adult Education, p. 7.

Williams, W. E. (1941). Adult Education: The British Institute and Its Experiments. *Manchester Guardian*. 1 February, p. 4.

Williams, W. E. (1942). *Letter from W. E. Williams to Kenneth Clark*. 25 June. Kenneth Clark papers: TGA 8812/1/1/14/235, Tate Gallery Archive, London.

Williams, W. E. (1946). Art Gallery for All. *Penguins Progress*, July, pp. 46–47.

Williams, W. E. (1949). *Letter from W. E. Williams to Allen Lane*. 21 July. Allen Lane files: DM1819/22/3/1/20, Penguin Archive, University of Bristol.

Williams, W. E. (1956). *The Penguin Story*. Harmondsworth: Penguin.

Williams, W. E. (1963). The Penguin King. *New Society*, 19 September, p. 11.

Williams, W. E. (1970). *A History of Penguins*, October. [Unpublished manuscript]. Penguin Books. Historical files: DM1294/14/1/48/1, Penguin Archive, University of Bristol.

Williams, W. E. (1971). The Pre-history of the Arts Council. In E. M. Hutchinson, ed., *Aims and Action in Adult Education 1921–1971*. London: National Institute of Adult Education, pp. 18–23.

Williams, W. E. (1973). *Allen Lane a Personal Portrait*. London: The Bodley Head.

Young, E. (1952). The Early Days of Penguins. *The Book Collector*, 1(4), 210–11.

Secondary Sources

Artmonsky, R. (2007). *Art for Everyone: Contemporary Lithographs Ltd*. London: ACC Art Books.

References

Blackburn, D. (2020). *Penguin Books and Political Change: Britain's Meritocratic Moment, 1937–1988*. Manchester: Manchester University Press.

Berthoud, R. (2003). *The Life of Henry Moore*. London: Giles de la Mare.

Button, V. (1993). Spreading the Word. In J. Lewison, ed., *Ben Nicholson*. London: Tate Gallery, pp. 63–69.

Calder-Marshall, A. (1947). *The Book Front*. London: The Bodley Head.

Canovan, M. (2005). *The People*. Cambridge: Polity Press.

Carney, M. (1995). *Britain in Pictures: A History and Bibliography*. London: Werner Shaw.

Chibnall, S. (1995). Pulp verses Penguins: Paperbacks Go to War. In P. Kirkham and D. Thoms, eds., *War Culture: Social Change and Changing Experience in World War Two Britain*. London: Lawrence & Wishart, pp. 131–49.

Craker, T. (1985). *Opening Accounts and Closing Memories: Thirty Years with Thames and Hudson*. London: Thames and Hudson.

Feather, J. (2006). *A History of British Publishing*. Abingdon: Routledge.

Fieldhouse, R., ed. (1996). *A History of Modern British Adult Education*. Leicester: National Institute of Adult Continuing Education.

Flynn, R. (2012). Archiving the Artist: The Graham Sutherland Collection at Amgueddfa Cymru, National Museum Wales. PhD thesis, University of Bristol.

Foss, B. (1991). Message and Medium: Government Patronage, National Identity and National Culture in Britain, 1939–45. *Oxford Art Journal*, 14(2), 52–72.

Foss, B. (2007). *War Paint: Art, War, State and Identity in Britain 1939–1945*. London: Yale University Press.

Fuller, P. (1988). The Visual Arts. In B. Ford, ed., *The Cambridge Guide to the Arts in Britain*, Vol. 9. Cambridge: Cambridge University Press, pp. 99–145.

Halliday, N. V. (1991). *More than a Bookshop: Zwemmer's and Art in the 20th Century*. London: Philip Wilson.

Hare, S., ed. (1995). *Penguin Portrait: Allen Lane and the Penguin Editors 1935–1970*. London: Penguin.

Haskell, F. (1987). *The Painful Birth of the Art Book*. London: Thames and Hudson.

Hinton, J. (2013). *The Mass Observers a History, 1937–1949*. Oxford: Oxford University Press.

Holman, V. (1993). Framing Critics: The Publishing Context. In M. Gee, ed., *Art Criticism since 1900*. Manchester: Manchester University Press, pp. 68–81.

Holman, V. (1999a). Art Books against the Odds: Phaidon in England 1938–1950. *Visual Resources*, 15(3), 311–29.

Holman, V. (1999b). Art Books in World War Two: A View from the Archive. *Art Libraries Journal*, 24(2), 12–15.

Holman, V. (2005). Carefully Concealed Connections: The Ministry of Information and British Publishing, 1939–1946. *Book History*, 8, 197–226.

Holman, V. (2008). *Print for Victory: Book Publishing in England 1939–1945*. London: British Library.

Holman, V. (2024). *Peter Gregory: Publisher and Patron of Modern British Artists*. London: Lund Humphries.

Joicey, N. (1993). A Paperback Guide to Progress: Penguin Books 1935–c.1951. *Twentieth Century British History*, 4(1), 25–56.

Joicey, N. (1995). The Intellectual, Political and Cultural Significance of Penguin Books 1935–c.1956. PhD thesis, University of Cambridge.

Keir, D. (1952). *The House of Collins*. London: Collins.

Kells, S. (2015). *Penguin and the Lane Brothers: The Untold Story of a Publishing Revolution*. Collingwood: Black.

Lake, M. (2014). *The King Penguin Series: A Survey*. London: Penguin Collectors' Society.

Lambert, J. W. and Ratcliffe, M. (1987). *The Bodley Head, 1887–1987*. London: The Bodley Head.

LeMahieu, D. L. (1988). *A Culture for Democracy: Mass Communication and the Cultivated Mind in Britain between the Wars*. Oxford: Clarendon Press.

Leventhal, F. M. (1990). The Best for the Most: CEMA and State Sponsorship of the Arts in Wartime, 1939–1945. *Twentieth Century British History*, 1(3), 289–317.

Lewis, J. (2005). *Penguin Special: The Life and Times of Allen Lane*. London: Viking.

Llewellyn, S. and Liss, P., eds. (2016). *WW2 – War Pictures by British Artists*. London: Liss Llewellyn Fine Art.

Lloyd Jones, L. (1985). Fifty Years of Penguin Books. In Penguin Books, ed., *Fifty Penguin Years: Published on the Occasion of Penguin Books' Fiftieth Anniversary*. Harmondsworth: Penguin, pp. 83–84.

Malvern, S. (2004). *Modern Art, Britain and the Great War*. London: Yale University Press.

Mandler, P. (2019). Good Reading for the Million: The 'Paperback Revolution' and the Co-Production of Academic Knowledge in Mid Twentieth-Century Britain and America. *Past & Present*, 244(1), 235–69.

McAleer, J. (1992). *Popular Reading and Publishing in Britain 1914–1950*. Oxford: Clarendon Press.

Mellor, D., Saunders, G., and Wright, P., eds. (1990). *Recording Britain: A Pictorial Domesday of Pre-war Britain*. Newton Abbot: David & Charles.

Meredeen, S. (2008). *The Man Who Made Penguins: The Life of Sir William Emrys Williams*. Stroud: Darien-Jones.

Morris, L. and Radford, R. (1983). *The Story of the AIA: Artists International Association 1933–1953*. Oxford: The Museum of Modern Art.

Morpurgo, J. E. (1979). *Allen Lane King Penguin*. London: Hutchinson.

Nyburg, A. (2014). *Émigrés: The Transformation of Art Publishing in Britain*. London: Phaidon Press.

Peaker, C. (2001). *The Penguin Modern Painters: A History*. London: Penguin Collectors' Society.

Pearson, J. (1996). *Penguins March On: Books for the Forces during World War II*. London: Penguin Collectors' Society.

Penguin Books (1985). *Fifty Penguin Years: Published on the Occasion of Penguin Books' Fiftieth Anniversary*. Harmondsworth: Penguin.

Powers, A. (2008). *Art and Print: The Curwen Story*. London: Tate.

Richardson, R. (1995). Closings and Openings: Leading Public Art Galleries during the Second World War. In P. Kirkham and D. Thoms, eds., *War Culture: Social Change and Changing Experience in World War Two Britain*. London: Lawrence & Wishart, pp. 87–97.

Rose, S. (2013). The Visual Arts in the BBC's 'The Listener', 1929–39. *The Burlington Magazine*, 155(1326), 606–11.

Rust, D. (2004). Penguin Books' Contribution to the Wartime Effort. *Penguin Collectors' Society Newsletter*, 62, 37–45.

Rylance, R. (2005). Reading with a Mission: The Public Sphere of Penguin Books. *Critical Quarterly*, 47(3), 48–66.

Schreuders, P. (1981). *The Book of Paperbacks: A Visual History of the Paperback*. London: Virgin Books.

Stephens, C. and Stonard, J.-P., eds. (2014). *Kenneth Clark: Looking for Civilisation*. London: Tate.

Tether, L. (2019). *The General Reader and the Academy: Medieval French Literature and Penguin Classics*. (Elements in Publishing and Book Culture). Cambridge: Cambridge University Press.

Trigg, D. (2017). Art Books for the People: The Penguin Modern Painters 1944–1959. PhD thesis, University of Bristol.

Weight, R. (1995). Pale Stood Albion: The Formation of English National Identity 1939–56. PhD thesis, University of London.

Weight, R. (1998). 'Building a new British culture': The Arts Centre Movement, 1943–53. In R. Weight and A. Beach, eds., *The Right to Belong: Citizenship and National Identity in Britain, 1930–1960*. London: I.B. Tauris, pp. 157–80.

Williams, R. (1989). Adult Education and Social Change. In Williams, R., ed., *What I Came to Say*. London: Hutchinson Radius, pp. 157–66.

Acknowledgements

This Element has its origins in my doctoral thesis on The Penguin Modern Painters. I am indebted to the Arts and Humanities Research Council for their generous support of the original research and I wish to express my gratitude to Dr Samantha Rayner for encouraging me to revisit the material and develop the present study.

I wish to thank Drs Grace Brockington and Stephen Cheeke at the University of Bristol for their professional guidance and encouragement during my initial studies. Thanks must also go to Simon Miles and Sarah Trigg for their invaluable comments and feedback that contributed significantly to the development of this study.

During the course of my research I have been greatly assisted by staff at numerous archives and libraries. I especially want to thank Michael Richardson and the late Hannah Lowery at the University of Bristol Special Collections for their generosity, expert advice and assistance in navigating the Penguin Archive. I am also grateful to Claire Brenard of the Imperial War Museum; the staff of the National Archives; the librarians of the Bodleian Library; Dr Martin Maw of Oxford University Press Archive, and the staff of the Tate Library and Archive for their dedicated assistance.

A number of individuals have provided valuable information or pointed me to useful sources. I would like to especially mention Tricia Passes, Mike O'Mahony and the late Michael Liversidge of the University of Bristol; Tim Graham, Joe Pearson and the late Steve Hare of the Penguin Collectors' Society; the help of Cathy McAteer, Alexandra Harris, Valerie Holman, Ana Nyburg, Frances Spalding, and James Stourton is also gratefully acknowledged.

I wish to extend my thanks to Joanna Prior, then Managing Director, Penguin General Books, for granting me permission to access the Penguin Archive, and in particular Kate Muldowney, Permissions and Content Licensing Assistant at Penguin Random House for granting permission to cite unpublished material written by former Penguin employees. All such extracts are reproduced by kind permission of Penguin Random House UK.

Acknowledgements

I am particularly grateful to the following individuals and institutions for permission to access and reproduce unpublished material: Nicky Sugar, Head of Special Collections, University of Bristol; Curtis Brown and the Trustees of the Mass-Observation Archive; Andrew Webb, Licensing Executive, Imperial War Museum; Bernard Horrocks, Head of Intellectual Property, Tate Gallery; Christine Teale, for permission to quote from the correspondence of her father, Sir Allen Lane; the Estate of Kenneth Clark c/o The Hanbury Agency Ltd., for permission to quote from the papers of Sir Kenneth Clark: all citations © Kenneth Clark, all rights reserved.

I dedicate this Element to the memory of Hannah Lowery (1969–2023), whose infectious passion for all things Penguin sparked my own interest in the history of this extraordinary publishing house.

Cambridge Elements ≡

Publishing and Book Culture

SERIES EDITOR
Samantha J. Rayner
University College London

Samantha J. Rayner is Professor of Publishing and Book Cultures at UCL. She is also Director of UCL's Centre for Publishing, co-Director of the Bloomsbury CHAPTER (Communication History, Authorship, Publishing, Textual Editing and Reading) and co-Chair of the Bookselling Research Network.

ASSOCIATE EDITOR
Leah Tether
University of Bristol

Leah Tether is Professor of Medieval Literature and Publishing at the University of Bristol. With an academic background in medieval French and English literature and a professional background in trade publishing, Leah has combined her expertise and developed an international research profile in book and publishing history from manuscript to digital.

ADVISORY BOARD

Simone Murray, Monash University
Claire Squires, University of Stirling
Andrew Nash, University of London
Leslie Howsam, Ryerson University
David Finkelstein, University of Edinburgh
Alexis Weedon, University of Bedfordshire
Alan Staton, Booksellers Association
Angus Phillips, Oxford International Centre for Publishing
Richard Fisher, Yale University Press
John Maxwell, Simon Fraser University
Shafquat Towheed, The Open University
Jen McCall, Central European University Press/Amsterdam University Press

About the Series

This series aims to fill the demand for easily accessible, quality texts available for teaching and research in the diverse and dynamic fields of Publishing and Book Culture. Rigorously researched and peer-reviewed Elements will be published under themes, or 'Gatherings'. These Elements should be the first check point for researchers or students working on that area of publishing and book trade history and practice: we hope that, situated so logically at Cambridge University Press, where academic publishing in the UK began, it will develop to create an unrivalled space where these histories and practices can be investigated and preserved.

Cambridge Elements ⁼

Publishing and Book Culture

Publishing and Book History

Gathering Editor: Andrew Nash

Andrew Nash is Reader in Book History and Director of the London Rare Books School at the Institute of English Studies, University of London. He has written books on Scottish and Victorian Literature, and edited or co-edited numerous volumes including, most recently, *The Cambridge History of the Book in Britain, Volume 7* (Cambridge University Press, 2019).

Gathering Editor: Leah Tether

Leah Tether is Professor of Medieval Literature and Publishing at the University of Bristol. With an academic background in medieval French and English literature and a professional background in trade publishing, Leah has combined her expertise and developed an international research profile in book and publishing history from manuscript to digital.

ELEMENTS IN THE GATHERING

Publication and the Papacy in Late Antique and Medieval Europe
Samu Niskanen

Publishing in Wales: Renaissance and Resistance
Jacob D. Rawlins

The People of Print: Seventeenth Century England
Rachel Stenner, Kaley Kramer and Adam James Smith *et al.*

*Publishing in a Medieval Monastery: The View from
Twelfth-Century Engelberg*
Benjamin Pohl

Communicating the News in Early Modern Europe
Jenni Hyde, Massimo Rospocher, Joad Raymond, Yann Ryan,
Hannu Salmi and Alexandra Schäfer-Griebel

Printing Technologies and Book Production in Seventeenth-Century Japan
Peter Kornicki

Unprinted: Publication Beyond the Press
Daria Kohler and Daniel Wakelin *et al.*

Mudie's Select Library and the Shelf Life of the Nineteenth–Century Novel
Karen Wade

Transnational Crusoe, Illustration and Reading History, 1719–1722
Sandro Jung

Art Books for the People: The Origins of The Penguin Modern Painters
David Trigg

A full series listing is available at: www.cambridge.org/EPBC

Made in the USA
Monee, IL
03 May 2026

49437539R00056